Father Manning, who was born in Muncie, Indiana, joined the Divine Word Missionaries in 1955. After his ordination, in 1969, he taught at Verbum Dei High School, Watts, California, was a pastor, and since 1972 has been the West Coast Vocation Director for the Divine Word Missionaries. As well as degrees in philosophy and theology, Father holds a master's degree in Fine Arts from Catholic University, where he specialized in dramatic writing. He has taught in the areas of journalism, English, speech and religion, and has written for magazines and television.

PARDON
MY LENTEN
SMILE

PARDON MY LENTEN SMILE!

(Daily Homily-Meditation Themes for Lent)

MICHAEL MANNING SVD

ALBA · HOUSE   NEW · YORK

SOCIETY OF ST. PAUL, 2187 VICTORY BLVD., STATEN ISLAND, NEW YORK 10314

Library of Congress Cataloging in Publication Data

Manning, Michael J 1940-
    Pardon my Lenten smile!
    1. Lent-Meditations. 1. Title.
BX2170.L4M36   242'.34   75-37881
ISBN 0-8189-0325-2

Imprimi potest:
Francis Shigo, S.V.D.

Imprimatur:
+ Leo T. Maher
Bishop of San Diego
December 3, 1975

*Designed, printed and bound in the United States of
America by the Fathers and Brothers of the Society of St. Paul,
2187 Victory Boulevard, Staten Island, New York, 10314,
as part of their communications apostolate.*

1 2 3 4 5 6 7 8 9 (Current Printing: first digit).

INTRODUCTION

Smiling should be a natural part of our Lent! As we draw closer in love to Jesus, He's going to give us the strength to stop doing things harmful and start doing what He's calling us to. Moving in this new power we're going to experience a new freedom and a fresh growth. So why not smile?

The book is aimed toward those who are looking for a fresh application of the scriptures for each day of Lent. This includes priests preparing their daily homilies and all Christians looking for a new direction in prayer.

The topics for each homily came through my prayer and reflection on each day's readings. The results took various forms: reflections from my personal experience, more formal type homilies, there's a short-short story, a parable and even a little play.

Special thanks to John Shevelin, SVD; Morris Cerullo and Patrick Connor, SVD. Their support and direction has helped me greatly. And then special thanks to Marge and Neila Alwardt for their generous assistance in typing. Scriptural quotations which are used are from the text of The New American Bible, copyright 1970 by The Confraternity of Christian Doctrine, Washington, D.C.

May your reading of these reflections draw you closer to Jesus. That would really make me smile!

Michael Manning, SVD

CONTENTS

PARDON
MY LENTEN
SMILE

ASH WEDNESDAY
Joel 2:12-18 / 2 Corinthians 5:20-6, 2
Matthew 6:1-6, 16-18

Jesus, here I go into another Lent, and I need Your help. All the past Lents that I've gone through have been good, but they haven't really touched the radical commitment I want to make of my life to You. Help me to love You more this Lent. Let today be the start of a deeper personal relationship that will give me a joy and happiness I've never thought possible before. You be the Center. Use Your power to transform my life. Jesus, I commit myself to You. From this moment on, I want to love You. Help me do my part. Thank You!

Jesus The Center

Here's a bit of the conversation I have with myself at the start of each Lent: "Well, here we go again! Another Ash Wednesday. Another Lent. What's it going to be this time? Popcorn? Favorite TV show? If you haven't come up with something yet, now's the best time. Perhaps a radical change is needed. Are you going to move away from that habit of sin you know you've been kidding yourself about all these years? Sure, this is the time to do it. Work on self control. Put discipline in your life!"

To be honest, this approach really doesn't do much for me. I've talked to myself like this so many times at the start of Lent. I wonder if it's worth going through all the struggle of missing my favorite TV show or not eating between meals when I know very well, in the back of my mind, a good week after Easter I'm going to be right back in the same rut I was before!

My spiritual life tends to be nothing but a big roller-coaster ride. Sometimes I'm gaining all kinds of victories in my life, but that inevitable backsliding comes in and I'm right where I was, on my back looking up at all the fading dreams of what might have been! Is Lent worth it? Why waste my time? Is there any way that this Lent could be different from the others? I would like today to be the start of something lasting. I would like to be able to put a new direction on that roller coaster ride and start making positive and lasting progress in my spiritual life.

Listen to me, will you? Listen very closely. I have the answer. There is no reason to take the roller coaster ride. This Lent can be the real beginning and it won't end at Easter or a week after or a month after or during the rest of our life. If we set our course right today, right now, we can experience victories in our spiritual life and in our striving for true happiness. The answer isn't "no candy" or making countless resolutions to break bad habits. The answer is Jesus Christ! Simple as that. We have to turn to Jesus with sincere trust and belief in His power. No more are we going to rely on our power. All that can produce is the monotonous roller coaster ride. Up until now, we've been like the silly dog that has exhausted himself chasing his tail. Panting and totally discouraged over not being able to reach our lasting goal, we have found the solution. In Jesus Christ we have power to do anything and everything.

He is the answer to a successful Lent and a successful rest of our life. From this moment on, we must turn and ask Him to make Himself the end and aim of everything. Not just some things, but everything we think or do or say. We will have to work very hard but we have a new source of success—Jesus Christ.

All we're doing is letting Him come in and take control. He has been waiting for this moment. Jesus is as near as the beat of our hearts. All we have to do is let Him take over.

The aim of this Lent has to be the development of a deep personal relationship with Jesus Christ. We must pray about this. Sharing in Mass each day is a beautiful means. Reconciling ourselves with God and our brothers and sisters in the parish through confession is a vital means. And yes, the fasting and sacrifice of giving up sweets and popcorn and eating between meals is all involved. But the heart and center of everything has to be our desire to commit ourselves in a deeper and more real way to the person of Jesus Christ.

You know what's going to happen? We're going to start

to have a joy in our life that we never thought possible. The commitment to and love of Jesus that is going to take control of our lives is going to make this Lent a joy! A real joy! Sure, smile. Why not? This Lent we're going to start gaining so many victories and we're going to start being so happy. No more down in the mouth discouragement because of spiritual break-down.

What really has me excited is that we can start something bigger than our transformation. When that fire of love starts to kindle in our hearts, it's going to be catching. People are going to get singed by the fire of Jesus' Holy Spirit burning in our eyes and voice and whole being. Our commitment to Christ will be the key that will open the Lord to others in our parish and community. Watch out when you're playing with fire in a dry field! There won't be fifty wet blankets (of the human variety) who will be able to dampen the fire of our love for Jesus which is going to spread far and wide.

Jesus, thank You for a new life and a new hope. Today is the start of a beautiful love relationship with You. Use Your power to help me to be centered on You. Thank You for loving me first!

THURSDAY AFTER ASH WEDNESDAY
Deuteronomy 30:15-20
Luke 9:22-25

Jesus, I want to be happy. Oh, not rolly-polly laugh-'em-up happy. I want a happiness that really is strong and lasting and true. I know that You are the only one that can give this. I know too that You have told me how to have that happiness: I have to lose my life in order to gain it with You. Ouch! The risk of letting go of my physical and material security and finding my strength in You is frightening. But Lord, I want to try. Give me the strength . With your help I can really be happy!

Losing to Find

If you asked me what is the most important thing in my life, happiness would have to be the answer. I really want to be happy: love, handball, movies, friends, liturgy, the sacraments, everything revolves around my desire to be happy. I don't think that I'm alone in this. I'm bothered, though, by what happiness means to so many people. I continually have to be careful that I don't fall into the trap of finding happiness only in sex, materials, and freedom.

You don't have to wander far into the world of TV soap operas, magazine racks, bill-boards, or movies to know that sex is one of the most important things for bringing us happiness. In a world of lonely, misunderstood, and frustrated people, this is the savior. This is what happiness is all about.

The next is materialism. We are bombarded so often with feelings of "not being with it" through clever advertising on TV, radio, and mail, and we soon find our quest for happiness taking the direction of a new car, a dish-washer, or a breath-freshener. Do you ever get the chance to watch any of those game shows on TV, usually in the morning? You should. Talk about happiness! And why? Well, someone just won $25,000 because he could spell the capital of Manchuria backwards faster than the other three contestants. Is this where happiness lies?

Then there's freedom. Do your own thing! That is fine. We all have to develop our talents in a spirit of freedom. But the freedom I see so often is a selfish freedom that disregards people who are in the way of my freedom. People are hurt. That can't be the happiness I'm looking for!

We who are followers of Jesus know that the most fundamental happiness we can find is in the difficult words of Jesus when He said that if we want to save our lives, we'll have to lose them. The most fundamental happiness comes from being willing to die that we may live.

Now we can die in various ways. A person who is on drugs dies when he goes through the agony of giving up the habit. He takes on a new life and is dead to his former self. I die when I reconcile myself with a person I've been at odds with. "It killed me" to go up to that person and tell him that I was at fault and would he please forgive me. What a fight to the death my pride puts up. Again, I die a thousand deaths before I have the courage to tell a person that I love him. The frightening aloneness of being made so vulnerable to rejection!

This death, though, is the key to our life in Christ and attaining happiness. We must continually die to ourselves and stop finding happiness in a selfish form of sex, or an ulcer-generating longing for more material gain, or freedom at all costs, even the cost of hurting a person we need to love.

That's why there aren't many Christians around. Who wants to die to be happy as Christ demands? It can't be easy taking this route. We'll be called foolish! I mean when other happiness is so readily available, why go through the anguish of dying? Through the power of Christ, though, we can weather any difficulty. With Jesus' support we can see beyond a passing happiness to a lasting and firm joy.

Once we embrace Christ's words and start dying to ourselves we will generate a deep personal love for Jesus, and pretty soon we won't be able to contain that love, and we'll be sharing our happiness with others.

FRIDAY AFTER ASH WEDNESDAY
Isaiah 58:1-9a
Matthew 9:14-15

Jesus, I want to fast this Lent. Now I don't want to do it just because others do. I want my fast to be the beginning of really coming to grips with myself. When I get hungry and tired I tend to take off some of the different masks I wear. Fasting reminds me of the serious job I have in coming closer and closer to You. Help me, will You? I want to grow from this fasting.

The Truth Through Fasting

Did you get a chance to see *Fiddler on the Roof*? I must have seen it twice on stage and twice at the movies.

One of the best scenes was the one where the leading man asked his wife, after twenty-five years, "Do you love me"? Isn't that something! I guess the reason the play was so successful was that it touched so many basic truths. And this sure was one. There are so many things that I do, day in and day out, without really meaning them. I have to continually come back at myself with the question, why? If I don't I become just like a robot. It's easy to get into a rut. Sure there was some meaning for what I did in the beginning, but, through time, if I don't take care, I just do things without a lot of meaning.

The readings today are talking about the importance of fasting—but not fasting without meaning. I really think that I could go all the way through a Lent doing my pet fast and really think I'm great while all the time I'm not growing deeper in the love I have for Jesus. Fasting has to have a true direction. Fasting has to be a shot in the arm that will help me renew my commitment to Jesus. He is what Lent is all about—not fasting. I have to be careful that I don't put the cart before the horse. The purpose of fasting is to deepen my love relationship with my God.

Fasting is like a cream pie in the face or a bucket of cold

water down the back on a brisk morning. Wakes you up! Stops you from settling down into the monotonous routine of life and puts a bit more vitality and meaning into everything that you do.

Once this foundation of deeper love with Christ is established, we start to move out to love others. Effective Christian action is a result of fasting.

In all of this we follow closely the life of Jesus. Before He began His work of bringing the good news of salvation to the world, He drew away from people in the desert and fasted. From this physical struggle with Himself through fasting, He was now able to move out and affect the world with His love.

As we try to follow closely the example of Jesus, we find that after His fasting, His love took a specific direction. Quite embarrassingly His involvement was a good bit less dignified and comfortable than my natural inclinations.

I would much rather deal with the "Brownies" and the parish little league team than minister to the people in the local brothel or the junkie who has a hundred dollar habit each day. The direction of Jesus' ministry was to prostitutes and sinners.

When I think of modern day Christian action, I'm reminded of a good friend of mine, a priest in Michigan. For a couple of years he had a really interesting ministry. He lived in a downtown parish. Most people came to the area from the suburbs at 9:00 A.M. and left at 5:00 P.M. Many, though, before they left, would stop at one of the numerous bars scattered throughout the parish. This is just where my friend began to minister. This tends to shake our image of priestly respectability, but what a strong imitation of Christ's concern for the poor and those in need of help. (The only problem was my friend doesn't like to drink!)

I think also of Mother Theresa picking up the dead and dying out of the gutters and garbage piles of Calcutta. I could think of ten other nicer needs I'd prefer to be involved with.

Another difficult place to minister is the jail in our town. And yet what a crying need is there for our presence as the

Body of Christ. Ah, and what about rest homes? The list of nitty-gritty involvement could go on and on.

Amazing, though, after I fast and deepen my relationship with Christ, my service of my brothers and sisters can go to some surprisingly beautiful extremes of love.

SATURDAY AFTER ASH WEDNESDAY
Isaiah 58:9b-14
Luke 5:27-32

Jesus, one of Your most beautiful gifts to me is the many close friends that I have. I thank You. They help me so much to grow. I can confide in them and know that they will not reject me. Help these people to strengthen my friendship with You. At times they seem so much more real than you. Help me to feel the strength of Your personal driving friendship through them. I so want You to be real in my life. I know that You will do all You can but give me a push every now and then so that I do my part!

Sharing the Truth of Ourselves

The experience is frightening. You are reaching out into a dim unknown. You are taking the risk of sharing with another person the truth about yourself, a fear, a part of yourself, a dream you have never dared tell anyone else. To you this is special and now you are willing to share it with another. If you had better sense you wouldn't do this! How do you predict this person's reaction? What if he does something stupid like destroy what you are offering? That would be bad enough, but worse, oh yes, far worse would be to have him notice the gift and respond with a smile. Not a happy smile, but a smile that indicates you are insignificant and silly.

But no! You've gone this far and for some crazy reason you won't go back. Something tells you the truth about yourself has to belong to someone else before it can be real.

Isn't that what makes friends grow? You take a precious dream or an embarrassing fear or a guilt-coated anxiety of the past and you give it to someone else and he takes it and doesn't laugh but accepts you.

A good friend is a person who has taken into his life the dreams and visions you have offered and made them a part of himself. Dropping our defensive masks and sharing the truths of ourselves is difficult. And yet, if we don't, we don't grow. We move only in a small circle of superficiality and sameness.

All this leads up to the important question right now in our lives: is our love for Jesus open and growing? For our love relationship with Jesus to grow, there has to be an honest sharing of our true dreams, fears, and weaknesses. We must not hold back.

There is a problem of playing games with the Lord. Bad games. We pretend when we deal with Him that we're really better than we are. We really don't like to come down on ourselves and admit that our life could be so much better.

You know what our problem is? We always do good. No, really, that's true. Everything that we do is done for a good reason. St. Thomas said something to the effect that man can never perform a conscious action unless good is the object of the action.

The problem is, all too often, the good we're concentrating on is only a tenth of the whole picture. Nine tenths is bad. When someone accuses us of doing something wrong we always have a come-back by making clear that the action was perhaps very bad but the aim of our intention was the tiny speck of good. "Hey, I'm not a bad person. I'm always doing good"!

Developing the intimacies of friendship with a person who is a walking model of goodness is difficult. What intimacies of precious value does a man who always does good have to offer? What a sad case!

What we have to do is realize that, sure, we always do good, but we don't always do the better. When I do this I have to take down the mask and admit I'm not so good. I have a weakness to share with others, a fear, a guilt, and a dream of a better me.

Let's stop the self-righteous game we're playing with the Lord and tell Him our weakness and need for Him. This is how our friendship with Jesus will grow: sharing the truth with Him and His body, the Church, and oh, with how much love He will accept us.

FIRST WEEK
OF LENT

MONDAY IN THE FIRST WEEK OF LENT
Leviticus 19:1-2, 11-18
Matthew 25:31-46

Jesus, You've come to show me the way to You. This way is
not vague. You've made things very explicit. Help me today to
examine honestly Your direction. Give me Your strength to act
as You want me to. And Jesus, may this help me to know You
and love you better.

The Key to Holiness

My cousin Alice was telling me that recently she mustered the
courage to approach a Jewish friend of hers with a question
that was really gnawing at her. Alice is a very convinced Christian
and has a hard time seeing why another wouldn't want to embrace the good news of Jesus as she has. When she acked her
Jewish feirnd why she hadn't accepted Jesus, she got a very
embarrassing answer, "If Jesus is the messiah, why hasn't He
made any difference in the world?" Ouch!

Now I'm sure that you'll agree with me that if we examine
the facts, Christ has made a profound effect on the world as
we know it today compared to two thousand years ago. But I
think that we have to listen more closely to what our Jewish
sister is saying.

The full sweep of the Christian message is certainly not being
effected the way it should in our day. If each Christian were
allowing Christ to move in his life the way Christ wanted to
move, our Jewish friend would have little support for not accept-
ing Christ.

Today's readings give us a strong reminder of what we must
do in concrete here and now terms if we want to live up to the
name of a follower of Jesus Christ. We have no cause to say
that the law of Christ's love is too nebulous or subject to the
whims of various theologians. God's words today are clear,
too clear to comfortably sidle away from their challenge.

In today's readings God gives us all the force of a one-two
punch. The Old Testament reading says explicitly what we must

not do and in Matthew we have the more mature and positive demands of what we *must do*.

Today's readings serve as a fine chance to sit back and examine our consciences. Slow down a moment and see where you need to stop some of the things that you are doing: stealing ... lying ... swearing ... defrauding ... cruelty...false judgments ... slander ... supporting the defenseless ... hatred...revenge...grudges.

As we grow older, being criticized and told not to do things becomes more and more difficult. This is especially true when we have a responsibility to correct children or employees. And yet this examination and honest listening to the Lord when He tells us to stop some of the things that we are doing is the key to growing to the holiness that the Lord is demanding of us.

Once we have come to grips with stopping the evil that we are doing, we must examine what positive things have to be done.

Am J feeding the hungry? As the bread winner of the family, am I conscientious in working to the fullness of my talents at my job so as to insure the security of food for my family? Am I perhaps on welfare and not striving as best I can to seek employment? As the cook in the family, do I strive to make all meals as special as possible? Am I conscientious about eating all food that the Lord has given me? Do I support the hungry around the world with my prayers and financial donations?

Am J giving drink to the thirsty? Do I make a point of offering a beverage to any guest in my home? If some dishevelled transcient were to come to my door asking for a drink, what would be my reaction?

Am J welcoming strangers? Do I make efforts to introduce myself to strangers moving into the neighborhood? What about at church? Am I too tied up with insecurity to reach out and introduce myself to someone I don't know at church? What about foreign students living in my home? What about welcoming foster children into my family?

Am J clothing the naked? How much of the clothing that I

have in my closet do I really need? When was the last itme able to dress as well as I can?

Am I comforting the ill? Do I take the time to find out who's sick in the parish and even if I don't know them too well, do I send them a "get well" card? Am I busy with too many other good things to visit the sick? When I visit the sick, do I give them the consolation of Jesus power by praying with them? Do I convey a spirit of strong faith in the healing power of Jesus when I visit the sick?

Am I visiting those in prison? Is there an old folks home in my neighborhood what I have never taken the time to visit? Although I don't know anyone there, have I visited the local jail and checked with the authorities to see if I could visit someone who never has visitors?

Christianity is more than a warm feeling you get when you attend Mass each Sunday. Christianity is also more than turning to Christ when tragedy strikes. Christianity is a day-in and day-out struggle to reach the holiness God has called us to. We must continually evaluate where we stand in the demands God is making in our commitment to Him.

A young man recently asked me a simple but terribly profound question, "How can I come to love Jesus more?" Jesus gives the key to the answer in today's gospel. When we feed the hungry, give drink to the thirsty, welcome the stranger, cloth the naked, comfort the ill and visit those in prison, we are rubbing shoulders with Jesus. And as we grow in the love of those that are in need, we grow in our love of Jesus.

TUESDAY IN THE FIRST WEEK OF LENT
Isaiah 55:10-11
Matthew 6:7-15

Jesus, I do so much talking. So much noise! Oh, not only coming from me, there's noise all around: there are cars, horns, radios and the TV! I wonder if I'm afraid to be quiet. Lord, help more quiet to come into my life. Let me learn how to listen to You. You know, I'm afraid that if I listen enough, I just might hear You talking to me, and in Your love You may want me to get lost in Your embrace. Help me to listen!

Listening to God

There are three possible ways we talk to each other—monologue, dualogue, and dialogue. MONOLOGUE: you've heard these people. They never let you get a word in edgewise. They're so excited about what they want to say and they've so developed the talent of non-stop lip action, you never get beyond "yes, but . . ." or "now if you ask me, I. . . ." Frustrating! The second is DUALOGUE: this is where both parties have the chance to get equal time on the floor, but when one is talking the other is so concerned about his response he can't get a chance to digest what's said. This isn't as frustrating as a monologue, but it sure is a waste of time.

The final one is DIALOGUE: it's a two-way street. There is a real sharing. You listen to the other and take what he says and build on the truth you both have. You both leave the conversation that much richer because of what the other person had to offer.

We have to be careful that our prayers to Jesus don't become so many monologues or dualogues. There has to be a real listening on our part. Yes, we have to listen to Him. How does He speak? In many ways.

The first reading today speaks of the word of God being effective. That's powerful. What effective means is that when God says something there is a creation. For example, in Genesis we hear the word of God going forth and all the world we know is created. Now what we need to do is realize that scripture is the word of God. God is actually speaking to us and that is power—the same power that created the Universe. St. Peter in his First Epistle says that the word of God is an indestructible seed. Whenever we hear scripture read, whether we're alert or ready to go off into a big snooze, a seed is put into our persons that can't be taken away. We are really dealing with power. A priest signifies that sacredness just before he reads the Gospel. He touches the book with a Sign of the Cross and then consecrates his mind, lips and heart. Jesus is actually speaking to me today, right where I'm sitting. It doesn't have to be just hearing the scripture read to us. Every time I read the word, that indestructible seed is implanted. God is not someone who is far away, He's right with us. He's alive. That's why Jesus Christ became man, to prove to us that God cares. Oh, if only we could realize His presence, even more than His presence, His power to effect the amazing promises He has made.

We do have to listen. We have to stop all the chatter on our part and put away all the cluttered-up concerns that take up so much of our waking hours. We have to really concentrate and allow the Lord to be more effective in our lives. We have to listen to get the full effect.

Scripture isn't the only way God speaks. He speaks through the Church, events of nature, people who confront us, who love us, and some who reject us. But there's one more of God's communication that really is difficult to come by in our age of noise. God speaks to us in silence. When we turn everything off and relax in His presence, with no noise, He starts saying things. Impossible? Difficult, I admit, but I hope not impossible. Try it. It's frightening. He actually communicates. Now I'm not saying that I'm hearing audible voices. No, not yet, but He does communicate. I've found that my reluctance to move into this quiet with God is caused by the fact that when He communicates, I don't like what I hear. He starts demanding of me an accounting of talents he has given me that I'd prefer not to take the bother to develop.

Let's concentrate on listening in our communicating with Jesus. What a key to growth and fullness of life that will be. I can't think of a better person I'd like to get a good word from.

WEDNESDAY IN THE FIRST WEEK OF LENT
Jonah 3:1-10
Luke 11:29-32

Lord, how I wish that I loved You more than I do. If I loved You the way that I should, I would be telling Your wonders to everyone that I meet. Look at me though. I'm so shy when it comes to telling other people about You. Oh, I'm fine when everyone knows that I'm a Christian and a priest on top of that. But what a chicken I am without my clerical shield. Give me courage, Lord. Help me to find You as the solution to the problems that people come to me with. Be my God and let me be Your Jonah, Your John the Baptist. Let me proclaim Your good news to everyone I meet.

Witnessing Jesus

Talk about being scared. I really was. Now the haunted house at Disneyland was bad and I'll never forget the first and last time I rode on a roller-coaster. But this time was even worse.

I was spending a couple days with my friend Bob in Palm Springs. Everything was going fine until Friday afternoon when he suggested, "Should be a lot of young people in the park tonight. Let's go down there and witness to them." I broke out in a cold sweat. I knew in a flash just what he meant, but I was hoping against hope when I asked, "Witness? What?" With no grace at all, my voice cracked on the last word. "Let's go tell them about Jesus." I wanted to explain as best I could to my Protestant friend that this kind of witnessing was all right for the separated brethren, but as a Catholic... well... you see... ah ... anyway I put it, things just didn't come out right. After all, here I am a priest, dedicated to Jesus. What could be more natural than to witness to Jesus? Drat! I didn't even have a Roman collar, let alone incense and a cope.

The rest of the afternoon was spent in abject terror. What was going to happen? I had frightening visions of being dragged off by my heels to the tune of "We Shall Overcome" as the remaining riot we instigated went flaying on. I was stuck. Aside from a sudden attack of debilitating dyspepsia, the evening would find me facing one of the greatest unknowns of my life: witnessing to Jesus to complete strangers.

You know what the worst part of my fear was? I was scared to death of what people would think of me. I really did some soul-searching that afternoon. What kind of dedicated Christian leader was I? Give me the right setting and the right people and the right climate and the right everything and I'm a fireball when it comes to preaching the Gospel. But to strangers? They might not like me. Worse yet, they might think I was one of those fanatics who's dedicated to Jesus.

Well, the time came. We walked a few blocks down the street and there before us was the enemy in full array. Well, it really wasn't quite that bad. As a matter of fact, they were pretty tame. There must have been ten teenagers sitting around. Nothing big, just sitting around talking about boy friends, girl friends, movies and records. On the way to the battle-field, we commandered another young Christian who played the guitar and had a nice voice.

The evening turned out to be quite innocuous. Our friend started playing some Christian songs on the guitar and soon everyone was around him, admiring first his voice and then asking about the message. It was as easy as falling off a log. Without any ranting and raving, I found I was comfortably talking about the love of Jesus and what He meant in my life. A couple of kids listened for a few minutes with quite a bit of interest, but then, with a polite smile, decided to move on. Before long, it was curfew time and a policeman came by and said we would have to move along. No bottles were thrown. Everyone got up and we headed for our different homes. A couple of the kids were walking with Bob and me. We shared superficial humor, humor that betrayed a new warm bond in Christ.

Someday I may talk in a gigantic church filled to the rafters, but it will never compare to the thrill of sharing Jesus with some complete strangers in Palm Springs.

I thought of this incident as I read the story of Jonah going into that town to preach repentance. Imagine the nerve! Imagine the trust in God it took! Just walking down the street shouting to everyone to repent. A modern advertising agent would shudder at the poor technique. But Jonah wasn't doing his thing. He was doing what the Lord wanted. And look what happened. Jonah's foolishness brought about the conversion of the whole city. Of course my experience was quite shallow compared to Jonah's, but I know now how important it is for me to grow in the courage to express my love for Jesus to others in and out of season. Jesus wants us to draw closer and closer in love to Him and I know that one of the signs of my willingness to love Him more is having the courage to share His Gospel with the people who come into my life.

Some of us are called to be more evangelical and some of us are called to a more difficult form of preaching: sharing our understanding of the love of Jesus with our husband, wife, sister, brother, or even our best friend.

So many times when people share their problems with us, we are quick to offer them all the knowledge we have about psychology, marriage-counseling, medicine or science. But are we just as quick to offer them the really powerful answer to any problem? Do we speak of the power and love of Jesus in our lives?

Some of the repentance the Lord is calling us to is to stop trusting in our powers and begin trusting in the Lord to move mightily through us.

THURSDAY IN THE FIRST WEEK OF LENT
Esther 14:3-5, 12-14
Matthew 7:7-12

Lord, sometimes when I pray, You really throw me for a loop! I don't know how to take You. I guess I want to know why it is that You put me into difficult situations where I need to turn to You for help. I really don't want to think of You as some insecure lover who wants me continually to prove my love for You. You don't have to do that. Why is it that You allow so much evil in my life and the world? Help me to understand You in this problem.

Our Freedom in God

One of my favorite writers is a Frenchman by the name of Charles Peguy. Pity I don't read French. I bet he's magnificent in the original. Charles was born late in the last century and died leading a group of men in a charge during the second World War. He was brought up as a Catholic, but when he went to the university he became involved in great social struggles and God didn't have much place in his life. He married another Socialist who was quite the avowed atheist. They had three children. Everything was going along quite well for them until suddenly Jesus Christ became the reality of his life and he knew that he had to return to the Church. The conviction was deep and sincere. The problem was that he couldn't share his faith with his wife and she refused to have the children baptized. Then the real tragedy struck. One of his children was dying. Charles pleaded with his wife to have the child baptized but she would hear nothing of it. Charles entered into one of the most frightening and, at the same time, most productive crises in his life. Deep in his bones was a dreadful fear of God. Jesus was a giant monster waiting on the brink to snatch his beloved child into everlasting torment. And Charles felt that he had no small part in this verdict. Friends tell of seeing Charles at this time walking up and down the aisles of buses, tears streaming down his cheeks, begging God to spare his son. What a frightening image he had of God.

From this terrible experience we have some of the most beautiful poetry written. The poems are entitled "God Speaks." The God who speaks is not the God of terror Charles felt deep in his guts, but the God of fatherly love and compassion that he wanted God to be.

Fortunately everything turned out well. The child recovered and eventually wife and children were baptized.

I introduced you to Peguy because he's helped me so much to understand how God in all His love and compassion could allow men to do the terrible evil that sometimes is inflicted on innocent and God-fearing people. What do you say to a person who doesn't believe in God and who shouts at you, "If there is a loving God, how could He ever allow six million Jews to be exterminated or all the rapes and murders that go on in the streets? Why are there so many divorces and abortions? Why so much injustice to the poor...?" If the definitive answer had ever been given, there wouldn't be a problem. But the evil we see and experience can gnaw at us or we can nervously ignore it. Peguy wrote a beautiful poem to explain. The God Peguy pictures in his poem on freedom is like a sensitive father who is teaching his son to swim. He's torn between letting his son go on his own to develop his confidence and muscles while at the same time caring very much that he doesn't get too much water in his mouth. He knows that he will never be able to learn if he doesn't swim, but unless there is some support, the boy is bound to drown.

God speaks:
When you love someone, you love him as he is.
I alone am perfect. It is probably for that reason that
I know what perfection is
And that I demand perfection of these poor people.
And how often, when they are struggling in their trials,
How often do I wish and am tempted to put my hand under
Their stomachs in order to hold them up with my big hand,
Just like a father teaching his son how to swim in the
    current of the river,

And who is divided between two ways of thinking.
For on the one hand, if he holds him up all the time
    and if he holds him up too much,
The child will depend on this and will never learn how
    to swim.
But if he doesn't hold him up just at the right moment
That child is bound to swallow more water than is healthy
    for him....
On the one hand, they must work out their salvation
    for themselves.
That's the rule. It allows no exception.
Otherwise it would not be interesting.
They would not be men....
Such is the mystery of man's freedom, says God,
And the mystery of my government towards him and
    towards his freedom.
If I hold him up too much, he is no longer free
And if I don't hold him up sufficiently,
I am endangering his salvation....*

*"Freedom" of BASIC VERITIES by Charles Peguy, translated by Ann and Juliem Green (New York: Pantheon Books). Reprinted with permission of the publisher.

FRIDAY IN THE FIRST WEEK OF LENT
Ezekiel 18:21-28
Matthew 5:20-26

Jesus, You came to bring love to the world. Knowing of this love You have for me, makes me happy. It makes me free. But I have to be honest with You. My love is not always as sincere as I would like. I say I love You and prove it in many ways, but then I ruin the whole picture by doing things I know I shouldn't. I think You'll ignore my sin because of the other acts of love I perform. Lord, don't let me take Your love for granted. Give me a healthy fear of You. Help me to feel Your strong demands on me to continually make my love as pure and undefiled as possible.

Fear The Lord!

When I was being educated in Christian grade schools, one very important aspect of my development was the fear of the Lord. The concept was quite sensible. God was something or someone, the difference seemed insignificant at the time, who was way out there doing all kinds of big things. He also was the one who was watching very closely to see how many smudges I had on my soul. (Ah, the famous blackboard circle with chalk marks placed here and there!) I learned to fear the Lord.

I went so far as to develop the dread disease of many seemingly righteous Christians, scrupulosity. Oh, and I had it bad. Saying the Our Father might take up to half an hour so that every word could be said with the meaning it deserved. God was not someone to be prayed to without concentration. Then there were the anguished hours of trying to examine my conscience and then hoping the confessor wouldn't mind my coming back again for Confession. After all, it was only thirteen minutes and forty-three seconds since my last confession. Oh, the memory of the time spent in such gigantic fear of the Lord!

I don't know when it happened. I suppose the more I came to know the Lord as a real person who meant something to me in my life, the idea of fear became less and less of a reality. I began to understand that my relationship with Jesus couldn't be based on fear alone but more on the demanding virtue of love. Love had so much more to make me grow than fear. Like a person freed from a prison, I was now able to start to fall in love.

But, as so often happens in life, I began to move from one extreme to the other. The God I "loved" was now a weak and ineffectual person. Anything was all right. The idea of Hell or my committing a sin unto death became out of the question. Occasions of sin became challenges to maturity. I claimed to be in love with a God who was such a nice guy that I could do anything and He didn't care.

I found it so easy to be satisfied with what I was doing and think that everything was fine. I'd sit back and enumerate all the fantastic things I was doing for the Lord. Like the poor publican looking at the sinner, I paternalistically looked at the rest of the world, wondering when it was going to get in step with the life I was so carelessly tripping.

Lent is a time of re-examining this danger. We need to step back and take a look at ourselves and admit there's a lot more that the Lord is requiring of us. Not only that, but we've got to stop some of the things we're doing! Right now! And unless we do, the consequences may be more than a gentle slap on the wrist. We need to awaken in ourselves a healthy fear of the Lord. Certainly love is important, but there might be something much more rudimentary that I have to come to grips with than love. I believe that along with experiencing the freedom of love, I have to bring my spirit and flesh into a fitting respect for a God of justice. Without this healthy fear and respect, love can become so much of an empty shell. I can be so happy with the good that I'm doing, and concentrating on this, I fail to realize that there are certain things that have to be taken under control before I can ever know what love is all about.

The fear of the Lord is what makes sure my love for Jesus doesn't become a distortion of selfish rationalization. The fear

of the Lord is like a boundary which enables me to move un-
encumbered into the depths of personal love of Jesus. The fear
of the Lord enables love to be forever true!

SATURDAY IN THE FIRST WEEK OF LENT
Deuteronomy 26:16-19
Matthew 5:43-48

Jesus, I want to love You and I want to grow in my love for others. One of the biggest difficulties I face in this is the fact I don't love myself the way I should. You know that, don't You? Oh, I put on a big show but deep-down there's that doubt about my goodness. I'm reluctant to share the deep down truths about myself with You or with others. I've got to grow in loving myself. After all, You love me. You love me so much that You've asked me to share Your life. Help me to love myself.

Importance of Loving Myself

When you add up all the facts, we human beings spend a great deal of time being rejected. I think that's why a lot of people don't think they're very good. Look at the facts: you start out in the womb. There you have everything a person could ask for: direct line to food, all the warmth you need—talk about the latest in water-beds! Then, just when you really love the situation, you get thrown out into the cold air. They grab you by the heels and with a rude awakening—you get a swift belt on the dignity! But that's just the start of the sorry road. You move into a half-way decent love relationship with this really great mother and father. They cuddle you, change you and make funny faces but then what? About a year later another baby comes on the scene and there goes all the attention and love! You get over that and start enjoying the home scene and then it's off to school. There you run into a bunch of people who treat you like a number. By the time you're a teenager all kinds of red blotches burst out all over your face and you fall madly in love with the girl in the third row. Mustering all the courage you can you ask her if she'd like to go to the movies. All you get is the most condescending smile imaginable. Crash! Eventually you start the whole process all over again with your own kids and what happens, they reject you because you're too out of touch with present times. Then the crowning point happens. You are sent to an old folks' home where, after all, you'll be most happy with people who understand you and can take care of you.

Along the way TV throws in its little helpers to shake your personal security by fostering doubts about the freshness of your breath and the odor of your body.

When I deal with people who are really struggling with a bad image of themselves, I ask them a very embarrassing question. "Name five things good about yourself." You wouldn't imagine the frightening responses. You know, there are many people who can't name one good thing about themselves.

Sometimes our Christian up-bringing didn't help this inability to love self. The magic word was humility. I think we need to take a new look at humility and see it quite simply as truth. You visit the house where the daughter has been practicing the piano for five years. Fine, you say, and ask her to play something and what response do you get? "Oh, I can't play!" People will smile and think what a humble child. Hog wash! That isn't humility. That's a lie. Humility means knowing who you are, strengths and weaknesses, and finding yourself good because of it. If you have a talent, you must love yourself and use it.

How does a person get over these negative feelings about self? The most lasting and fundamental way is experiencing the fact that Jesus accepts you right now for who you are. He looks at you with your weakness and strength and says, "I like what I see. You're my kind of people."

This experience of being accepted is hard to program. It certainly takes openness on our part but it is ultimately a gift of God. At some moment in our lives we know beyond a shadow of a doubt that we are accepted by God. He believes in us. From that moment on, our life takes a new direction. This is what Baptism and its continual renewal is all about. In the midst of weakness and rejection, a power outside of us says, "you are accepted," and from then on love takes on meaning.

I can love myself, and once that happens I am free to sincerely love others. My relationship with God has a brand new super-highway of intimacy opened up. . . .

Suddenly, Jesus' words "love your neighbor as yourself" take on a new and lasting meaning.

SECOND WEEK
OF LENT

MONDAY IN THE SECOND WEEK OF LENT
Daniel 9:4-10
Luke 6:36-38

Jesus, You remind me, today, to be careful that I don't judge others. I'm really at fault here! I know a person for a while and I can predict just how he's going to act. Very subtly, I tell him what I think he can do. Most of the time he acts accordingly. Help me to see people as surprises. Help me to open up my expectations and let them surprise me with their beauty which is far beyond my narrow judgments.

People as Surprises

We're upset when people try to put us into a box. And yet, we're all continually putting people in boxes. I don't mean the cedar kind that go six feet under, or the kind you get at the grocery store. I'm talking about the boxes whose walls are the expectations and judgments we make about how people will act.

I find this so very true especially with people I've known for a long, long time. I know them in and out. I can predict any action they may take. With some it may be an act of knowing love and with others it becomes a terrible restriction that's very hard to break through. Boxes are what prejudice is all about. We see a person with a certain ethnic characteristic and before we even know him we've put him into a box of our expectations. Then we castigate him for never getting out of the stereotype into which he has been nailed.

This is quite natural. Putting people into a box takes less effort than going through the risk of loving a person as an individual rather than a thing. This is fine if we're satisfied with stagnation. I'm much more enthusiastic about growth.

The key to doing away with boxes in our lives is to have an open mind and let everyone we meet, no matter how long we've known them, be a surprise.

Be A Surprise!

You show me a person who doesn't like a surprise and I'll show you a person who's a complete bore. What I'm proposing is exciting! Everyone you meet, from this moment on, is going to be a surprise. Life will take on a new direction!

This is what following Jesus is all about: excitement, newness, life, growth and surprises. When we become a follower of Jesus, we start on a road which will continually allow us to grow and develop in a new way the talents the Lord has given us. The problem is that many times the Lord calls us to this growth through the direction of other people. So many people are wet blankets when it comes to my going beyond what they think I'm capable of.

We're like icebergs, one seventh of us is all that others see. What about the hidden depths of potential that come out in tragedies? I've heard of a man who, in a moment of panic lifted a burning truck to free a child.

We can begin to usher in the kingdom of God in our time if we break down the walls we've put up around the members of our family and friends. Do it! Free people from your limiting expectations. Watch what happens. They'll blossom in a way you never thought possible. Encourage them to go beyond the world in which they've gotten bogged down. They will start to undertake tasks they never thought possible. They'll start to love people, confront injustice, curb sin and grow deeper and deeper in personal love of Jesus.

Boredom and sameness are such big factors in a world that can't find happiness. We have to burst into the world with the freshness and hope of Jesus and shake up everyone with surprise, after surprise, after surprise. What a valuable key to attracting more people to Jesus. We make Him real by giving the world His newness and life.

What a wonderful surprise Jesus is. To those who are lost, sad and without hope, God becomes man and offers each of us brotherhood with Him and everlasting life! Who would have imagined!

TUESDAY IN THE SECOND WEEK OF LENT
Isaiah, 1:10, 16-20
Matthew 23:1-12

Jesus, being a priest is a heavy responsibility, frightening in a way. I'm called to witness to the people of God and direct them in Your truth. That takes a lot of preaching. So many times my preaching has been empty. I've just gone through the motions. Many times I am the one who should be listening to what I'm saying. I am the one who needs to change my life. Help me, Jesus, to be genuine. Don't let me be a big front, but rather a person who is really in love with You and anxious to share this love with my brothers and sisters. Make me true in everything I do!

The Key to Effectiveness in Witnessing

Jerzy Grotowski is the director of a group of actors in Poland. He is in a class all by himself. His actors may work on a play for a year or longer before they perform. Now it's not that these actors take a long time to remember their lines, or the scenery is difficult to construct, or that they can't get anyone to come to the plays. Grotowski believes that the heart of a dramatic performance is the actor's ability to say the truth about himself. He believes when this is expressed, people in the audience are forced to face the truth in themselves. Did you get what I'm saying? I think it's really important, especially, for a priest who is so frequently in the pulpit.

Every time you are really moved by a good actor, Grotowski believes, it isn't techniques of gestures and voice projection and inflection. What makes an actor good is that he knows a truth about himself. He then can express this through his acting art. You and I seeing him on stage are really forced, because of his honesty, to see the truth about ourselves.

An actor's knowledge about truth doesn't come easily. There is a great deal of introspection and meditation before the actor knows this truth. This is why some actors take over a year before they can step on stage.

When I heard about Grotowski, I couldn't help but make

the comparison between a good actor and me the priest. If
I really want to be effective in my preaching, it's not going
to be because of the clever ideas or the booming voice or the
dramatic pauses. What I need to work on is knowing the truth
as I've experienced it in my life, then, as honestly and simply
as possible, use my homilies as a vehicle of this truth. This is
how I'll affect the lives of others. My parishioners will be exposed to my expression of the truth, and my words will become
a kind of catalyst which forces them to recognize the truth about
their own lives.

As a priest, I must preach Jesus Christ. This has to be my
primary concern in my truth quest. I must search and medi-
tate, pray, and live the Gospels to the hilt to make Jesus Christ
real in my life. My homilies will be the expression of the
truth of this reality. Then, right along with what Grotowski
says, I will force my hearers to awaken the Jesus reality in
their lives.

Jesus warns us priests today that we have to be careful to
practice what we preach. Unless we touch this truth of the
personal love relationship with Jesus in our lives and then express it through our homilies, we're going to be so much empty
air. What a frightening responsibility!

What do you do if you're not a preacher? What do you
do if the homilies at Mass are a complete bore and there is
no personal truth being expressed by the priest? Well, the road
runs both ways. If you can touch the truth of your life and
express it, you can move your priest. Pray much to know the
truth about your experience of Jesus and then quite simply
express this to your priest. According to Grotowski, if you
are speaking a truth in your life, you will force the priest to
face and know truth in his life. This might not happen right
on the spot. With some, truth grows upon reflection. But you
have put the seed in someone's heart. He will be a new person
because of your truth.

Priests, let us pray and struggle to know the truth in our
lives and to have the courage to express this truth. This is

how we're going to move the people that we thought were totally bogged down. If we don't, people are going to look for the truth elsewhere, perhaps from a rock singer, a movie star or politician and not from Christ.

WEDNESDAY IN THE SECOND WEEK OF LENT
Jeremiah 18:18-20
Matthew 20:17-28

Jesus, when I read Your good news to follow You through Your life, I see You continually running into opposition. You made so many people feel uncomfortable by Your way of dealing with them. What You did was very simple. You loved. That's why people persecuted You and eventually put You to death. You wouldn't be tied down to doing things, "the way they've always been done!" You loved the individual who was before You. Help me to do what You did. Yes, I know there will be persecution just like You experienced, but I want to be close to You!

Taking A Stand

A Man For All Seasons was a play about the life of St. Thomas More. This was the best dramatic movie that I've ever seen. It has been many years now since I saw it, but there is one part that always comes to mind when I think about the importance of persecution as a way of life of a follower of Jesus.

More was the Chancellor of England. By profession he was a lawyer. He loved his king. He loved his country and he loved its laws. Then a terrible dilemma materialized when the King decided to move away from allegiance to the Pope in Rome. What was More to do? He loved his country and the King, but he also loved his Church and its roots in Rome. He was faced with two deeply personal loves and yet, he couldn't have both. It wasn't that there weren't problems on both sides. The King he loved was ruthless and not faithful in marriage. But then too, the Church he loved was full of all kinds of sinful men. What was he to do?

Thomas More is special to me because he didn't take a stand with the blast of a trumpet. He made his decision to remain faithful to the Pope. However, he strove by might and main to find some legal solution that his lawyer mind could come up with to allow him to serve both. In a beautiful scene in the sweating walls of the Tower of London, his wife visits her prisoner husband and asks why he won't just sign the statement of allegiance to the king and come back to the comfort of his home and family and spend the rest of his life doing good. With anguish on his face, More cries from the guts of his being that he is not the stuff of martyrs. He doesn't know for sure if he's doing the correct thing. There is good on both sides, but what he knows is that he has to take a stand. This man of questions and doubts did take a stand and was beheaded for something he surely believed in. There was a great deal of love also for what he opposed so strongly.

How often, in my youthful enthusiasm, I want to go against the tide and take a stand. I will no longer vacillate. I know what has to be done. I step out in my determination and what happens? I'm bombarded, not with the glory that is belonging to the martyr, or the champion of right, but with the quiet and convincing logic of the other side. Blah! Or with the knowing smile of the 'mature' person who has seen the same approach several times and knows, in the long run, there isn't any use being different. You know who these wet blankets are? Not the stranger. The primary wet blankets to my standing up for what I believe, I thought I believed, are the people closest to me, friends and relatives. And what's the result? Usually, with all the dignity I can muster, I place my tail securely between my legs, give a lick to my wounded pride and retreat to quiet mediocrity.

Now we have to be careful when we're talking about standing up for what we believe. We have to be people who listen. I'm not advocating the "bull in the china shop" scene where we're different because of some feeling of insecurity. Our example of being different has to be Jesus. With Jesus, our reason for being different must be love.

Look at just a few of the things Jesus did that caused Him persecution: He confronted the injustice of the religious leaders, the Scribes and Pharisees, "how dare you question a holy man of God?" He loved the poor, "they need a kick in the pants to stop being so lazy." He loved prostitutes, "you know what will happen if you hang around them too long!"

Our leader Jesus spent His whole life suffering persecution because He loved. We, who are His Body in the world today, must continue His mission. Being a Christian isn't easy, for we will have to be continually choosing between two goods. The heart of being a Christian is not fluctuating between decisions we're not sure of, but, eventually, coming to a stand and doing so out of love.

THURSDAY IN THE SECOND WEEK OF LENT
Jeremiah 17:5-10
Luke 16:19-31

Jesus, I'm so impatient. I'm spoiled by all the instant gadgets on the market. And this makes me think that You have to be that quick. Help me to understand how You work in Your time in my life. When I get impatient with You, help me to relax and trust. You have a power based on a deep personal love for me. Help me to keep my eye on Your power and not so much on the quick happiness the world offers me. Let me rest in Your time.

God's Time, Not Ours

We live in an instant world: instant potatoes, instant photographs, and instant TV pictures. We can cover the breadth of the country in four hours on commercial planes. Phone calls can reach anywhere and we can talk right now with anyone.

We tend to be impatient people. We get so into the pattern of instantaneous results that when we can't obtain things as quickly as we'd like, ulcers and heart conditions come on the scene.

God often doesn't seem to fit into our instantaneous notions of how life should run. So often He seems to take His good time. If that isn't enough, sometimes He seems to disappear from the picture entirely. God is so frustrating at times because He doesn't act in the manner we expect or with the speed we demand. Our dealings with God are similar to those of the young teenager who wants, more than anything, to be grown up right now. But life doesn't work that way. Growing up comes in time and oh, the time can seem interminable.

Sometimes God works fast and that's a delight to our impatient mind. But often He works in His own inscrutable time. To Jesus the kingdom of God was like a mustard seed that starts as the smallest of seeds, but grows, in its own slow time, into a big tree where birds come to nest. The story of Lazarus in the Gospel of today is a good example. Here he was, living his whole life in very hard times, begging for everything he had. How impatient he must have been to have the comfort and satisfaction of the rich man.

The Lord blessed Lazarus in Eternity but that was after many difficult years when God's seeming indifference glared in his life. "Please God, You have the power. You know that I'm basically a good person. Why wait? Get things done!"

So many times, I'm not able to see that there is a loving God directing my life with an intelligent love that is beyond my comprehension and time schedule.

There are two alternatives to our dilemma. We can stomp our feet and shake our fists at God. We can break out with a bad case of anxiety or we can relax and trust. It seems un-natural to talk about relaxing and trusting. You feel anxiety is the natural way of acting.

I really don't think that God wants me to have a nervous breakdown as I frantically run around, trying to manage my ilfe. Anxiety and nervous breakdowns are the result of not realiz-ing that in God we are dealing with a gigantic amount of power. There is more power in God than can be generated by the greatest man-made atomic reactor. That power is not as cold and impersonal as the gigantic reactor. No, the power we have in God is a power directed to us with love.

How do we activate that power which so far surpasses any power we've ever come up against?

Interestingly enough, the answer is instantaneous. We can have the power of God in our hands right at this moment. What do we do? Let go! Right now! Do it! Let go of all the controls you've been feverishly manipulating up till now. In a word, trust. Trust that God is present with you right now. He loves you right now. He is willing to let your anxieties be taken away by reaching out in hopeful trust to Him. The prayer we say after the Our Father at Mass becomes a possibility and not a fairy tale pipe dream. "Protect us from *all* anxiety."

We have to move from the basis of our trust in material things: cars, Bell Telephone and TV commercials, to the relaxation of trust in a God who loves us personally and who has the power far beyond our fondest dreams.

The love of Jesus helps us move our priorities from seeking happiness in instantaneous materialism to the power of God moving in personal, growing love in our lives.

FRIDAY IN THE SECOND WEEK OF LENT
Genesis 37:3-4, 12-13, 17-28
Matthew 21:33-43, 45-46

Jesus, when You called me to follow You, You called me to something really great. My life is now involved with something new and fresh. The key to allowing this to happen is doing just what Joseph did in today's first reading. I have to dream. A dream is a key to greatness. No, not my personal greatness, but the greatness of Your Kingdom. Teach me to dream more. Help me continually to be able to have a vision beyond the here and now. Give me the dream of how I can help to make Your Kingdom come.

Dreamers

Walter Mitty is a laughable creation of James Thurber. Mitty certainly wasn't much to look at, being slight of build, nervous, awkward and very ineffectual. He was a sad case. He was continually being hen-pecked by his domineering wife. But Mitty wasn't as dumb as he looked. He was able to escape from his dreary existence by an ingenious means. He would dream. Thurber's account of Walter Mitty's world is hilarious. Mitty would be driving downtown with his wife pestering him every inch of the way. Suddenly an airplane would fly overhead and that was all Mitty needed to escape. Suddenly, he was the commander of a gigantic bomber which was on the most important mission of the war. Despite having to fly through a hurricane, he astonishes all the crew members with his coolness and bravery under pressure and delivers the bombs and, of course, wins the war single-handedly. Another time his wife is pestering him to go to the doctor to see what's wrong with him and through the magic of dreams he becomes a world-renowned surgeon saving an ailing admiral.

Walter Mitty is fun to read about and although he might be an exaggeration, we know how true his escape into fantasy is with each of us now and then. Whenever we're tied down into a situation that's too difficult, dreams are a natural recourse.

Unfortunately, dreams have developed a bad name. Because they aren't real, they're considered a waste of time. They might be good for a laugh, but a mature person is continually trying to get away from dreams to effective here and now activity. Along with being a waste of time, dreamers are dangerous. Dreamers never are satisfied with the way things are and are always offering ideas on how things can change. They always seem to be bucking the status quo. People spend a long time trying to get things settled down and organized and then a dreamer comes along and wants to disrupt things.

Perhaps we should start to encourage more dreaming. I don't mean the Walter Mitty brand of dreaming. This was selfish escape. I'm talking about dreaming that fosters hope and the prospects of growth in the future. I'm talking about people being encouraged to express their dreams of a better world.

Joseph in today's first reading was a dreamer. He could see beyond the present. As with most dreamers who have the courage to express their vision, he got into trouble. Jesus too was continually speaking of His vision of how things should be beyond the here and now. All of His Parables are based on a deep longing for His Kingdom to come. Again, as with Joseph, Jesus' vision got Him into all kinds of trouble. People in authority liked things the way they were, but Jesus kept prodding them onto greater perfection.

In today's Parable, the Kingdom is given to the one who can yield a rich harvest. That means growth and growth means continually moving from things as they are to things as they will be. Dreams are the stuff of which growth is made.

How we long for God to work His marvels in our life. And yet, unless we have the courage to dream and strive to make that dream real, we'll never know the marvels the Lord is wishing to work in our lives.

So, try it if you dare. Dream of a world that can be. Imagine how God's Kingdom of Love and Peace, Unity and Joy could exist in your life and then courageously do something to make that dream a reality.

SATURDAY IN THE SECOND WEEK OF LENT
Micah 7:14-15, 18-20
Luke 15:1-3, 11-32

Jesus, there are so many things that I have done in my past that I wish I hadn't. So many ideals I have of myself have fallen through because of my weakness. I know that You gave me talents and that I should be using them to make You more loved. I do have a lot of guilt about this. I'm ashamed of myself. Help me to know and experience Your forgiveness. You love me and want me to come to You, not dragging my feet with guilt, but with the freedom and happiness that can come only in being washed in Your Blood. Help me.

Lord, Free Me From Guilt

Benedict Arnold is a person our history books have put under the rug. My first real exposure to Arnold was several years back. There was an article about him in the encyclopedia. I couldn't believe my eyes when I read what he had done during the Revolutionary War. Yes, there was a great deal of disgrace connected with going over to the English near the end of the war. But what astounded me most were the facts of what he had done for the country up until the point of being a traitor.

Arnold was perhaps the most successful commander of men in the whole Revolutionary War. He had an uncanny ability to turn even the most depressing situation into a glittering victory for the Colonies. Twice he almost lost his right leg in battle. At one point, he was appointed Governor of the city of Philadelphia, certainly a center of the revolutionary effort. And had it not been for Benedict Arnold, a surprise attack by the British after the Battle of Saratoga would have turned the whole war around. Single-handedly he mustered soldiers and saved the victory. Just before he went over to the British, he was in command of West Point. General Washington had great respect and admiration for him.

The key to his success was his great enthusiasm for the Revolution and his love for his country. His men looked upon him as a leader for whom they would give their all.

The end of his life was very sad. . . . He died in London far from the country he had given so much. His name was one of disgrace in the Colonies and in England things were no better. No one would trust him.

Today's readings talk about exile. We see people away from the things that they know and love. They are alone and not finding the peace and love they want, much like Arnold in exile. This exile is a very real thing today too. There are many people who are in exile from the ideals they had when they were younger. They have made a mistake and now are alone in their guilt.

A psychiatrist once said that fifty percent of his patients could go home cured if they could do away with their feelings of guilt and experience the real meaning of forgiveness. I meet so many people who are spending all their time spinning their wheels in life being full of sorrow for past sins and not having time to grow in the many gifts the Lord has given them. They think more of the evil of their past rather than of the great work that lies before them.

In the confusion and depression that is associated with guilt, an awareness of one's complete futility comes to the fore. There is really nothing that I can do to lift this terrible burden off my back. I need help. I need someone greater than me to take all my guilt. This is where Jesus comes in with His sustaining power, because He is the Creator and Sustainer of everything that is in existence. If we could just let this settle into our bones. Jesus as the Creator is in the middle of everything that's happening. He has complete control. Since this is the case, He would be the best person to turn to and ask to have the burden of guilt taken away. This is just what He wants us to do. He has told us that He has come to take away our sins. This is why He died. He is just waiting for us to turn to Him and ask His help. With His loving power He can give freedom. He can give us the freedom from the guilt for the sins of our past life.

Think about this when you pray at the Eucharist. Pray

with trust and confidence when you say, "Lamb of God, Who takes away the sin of the world." Let this reality permeate your being.

The first step to forgiving yourself and then forgiving others for evil is realizing that God has forgiven you. How frustrated I would be if I were God and I had the power to give happiness and forgiveness to a person and that person never turned to me and asked for my help.

What strong security to know that like the father in the prodigal son story, God never lets up His vigil, hoping for my return to the peace and love of His embrace.

THIRD WEEK
OF LENT

MONDAY IN THE THIRD WEEK OF LENT
2 Kings 5:1-15
Luke 4:24-30

Jesus, You once said, "The man who has faith in Me will do the works I do, and greater far than these" (Jn 14, 12). That's a powerful statement. Lately, I've been hearing a lot about miracles being performed by men who are close to You. I shy away from this. I've become so imbued with the miracles of science and technology and the pride in my own ability that I'm afraid to admit that Your power is alive and real in my life in a way beyond my mechanical calculations. Help me to have faith in Your power in my life to perform miracles. Help me to be an instrument of the miracles of Your love.

Miracles Today

I was recently confessing to my Protestant friend Bob, that I have a hard time understanding all these fantastic miracles I hear about on TV. For some reason, all the Protestant Evangelists seem to be performing miracles. I told him that I doubted that God could be so liberal with His marvels. He put me back on my heels when he replied that when he was small, he never heard of miracles in his main-line Protestant church. The only miracles he ever heard of were those associated with the Catholics and started mentioning Lourdes, Fatima, and all the miracles associated with Saints.

That started me thinking. Miracles certainly are an important part of Catholicism. Of course, I know about the documented and tested miracles that happen in Lourdes. And then there was the miracle of the sun at Fatima which even atheists attested. Oh yes, and before the Church will beatify a person there have to be two miracles attributed to the Saint's intercession and two more before sainthood. Of course, there was the Sacrament of the Sick. How many times I had experienced a complete reversal in a patient's condition after the administration of the Sacrament. And as if that weren't enough, what I had been saying, without meaning, for such a long time at Mass became clear, ". . . I eat your Body. . . . Let it not bring me condemnation but health in mind and body." And then, immediately after: "Lord, I am not worthy to receive You, but only say the word and I shall be healed."

I turned to Scripture for understanding. There was no doubt that Jesus was continually working miracles. Everyone was being cured: the deaf, lame, blind, lepers, possessed, and even the dead were being brought to life. But . . . that was then and this is now. I kept telling myself that Jesus had important things to start in His day and the need for miracles such as He performed really wasn't part of His plan now. And I comfortably sat back, free from another responsibility. And then I read a verse from St. John. I must have read it many times but this time I found a new meaning. Listen: "The man who has faith in Me will do the works I do and greater far than these." That is shocking in its implications. The wonders that fill the Scriptures are things that should be going on today and to an even greater extent. Astounding!

This realization, put into practice, strengthened the bond of personal relationship I had with Jesus. I began confronting the mentally and physically sick who confronted me, not first with a psychologist and doctor and then prayer, but the other way around. I began to pray that the sick and disturbed people I met could have the full power of Jesus' healing help. And I began to pray with confidence and trust and thanksgiving that He would act. I didn't forget the psychologist or the doctor. They are part of God's action too. But I kept the correct order. I went first to where the real power is.

With my weak faith this was difficult, but I wanted to do all I could. My biggest fear was really hurting a person who had spent years trying to reconcile a broken spine with the will of God for her. Who was I to raise her hopes when in reality God might want her sick and broken?

I soon learned that the whole thrust of Jesus in Slripture is not toward sickness but health. He wants us to ask for healings. He wants us to have faith in Him, that He will use

His power, even at the risk of dredging up new ways of looking at sickness.

Healing comes in God's time and not ours. Some are instantaneous. Some happen, then relapse, and then come for good. Some take what seems an interminably long time. But healings happen whenever we pray.

Try to remember that the faith that's required is not in ourselves. That would lead nowhere. The faith we have is in the power of God to be able to do these things.

All miracles are so much sand unless they achieve the end for which they are performed: a deepening of the personal love relationship with Jesus. What a fright to see a cure and then find no change in the person regarding his relationship with Jesus.

TUESDAY IN THE THIRD WEEK OF LENT
Daniel 3:25, 34-43
Matthew 18:21-35

Jesus, I tend to pat myself on the back when it comes to forgiving people. There really aren't any people that I hold grudges
against and refuse to talk to. But You know what my problem is.
I get back at people who've hurt me, very subtly. I'm clever
about not forgiving. I've developed a mild condescending attitude
toward people who've wronged me. Sure, I forgive, but it's hard
for me to forget and really start off with a clean slate. Help me
to forgive and not get back at people with my petty hurt pride.

. . . As We Forgive Those

Strange how one person can change so much in just a few
years! Jerry Holdmann had. When he took over the job of head
counselor at "Camp Happy Days" twenty-three years ago, he
could be seen running and laughing and going along with the
childish pranks often more easily than the little boy campers.
This merriment didn't mean he wasn't running a tight ship.
Camp was for having fun and when a little boy became selfish
and didn't want to cooperate, Jerry came hard on him. Missing
Thursday night's movie was the worst punishment. Deep down,
the campers welcomed this discipline and knew that Jerry
punished because he loved them very much.

Tragically the love in Jerry began to dim five years ago
when the drastic change came in the camp. The spoiler was
organized Little League. The camp used to be only for boys.
Then baseball games began cutting into the boys' free time.
Numbers started dropping and dropping at the camp until the
owners from Los Angeles called an emergency staff meeting.
The resident nurse, Miss Caroline, was the one who made the
dastardly suggestion of turning the camp over to girls. Jerry
was vehement in his objection. But the owners were desperate
enough to give the girls a try and, wouldn't you know, the
scheme worked like a charm.

The tragedy of the switch was that Jerry could no longer

be head counselor as he had been for almost twenty years. His whistle of authority went to Miss Caroline.

He almost gave in his resignation, but then the thought of a summer without "Happy Days" was too frighteningly unfamiliar and lonely. Added to this was the desire to be around when the camp went back to boys as he felt sure it would. He wanted to do everything he could to hasten the return.

Because of his long history with the camp, Jerry was given the title of head gardener. Actually, there weren't any other gardeners because there wasn't even enough work for Jerry. He spent most of his time pushing stacks of pine needles and stray pieces of paper into garbage bags to be taken by the trashmen every Monday and Friday.

In the years since the switch, Jerry took on a gnawing bitterness toward the new campers and the staff. They were the cause of a situation he could never quite forgive them for. The thirty pounds he had put on since the change seemed to leave no room for the fun Jerry had been so full of. The high-pitched laugh that had been his hallmark didn't echo with glee through the mountains anymore. Jerry laughed all right, but with a mocking tone as twelve carefree six-year-old girls marched from archery to crafts and singing, "B-I-N-G-O, B-I-N-G-O, B-I-N-G-O, Bingo was his namO!"

"Silly song!", he'd mutter and then try and recall how much more fun the boys had. "They'd be having too much good solid fun to prance around singing prissy songs."

He soon found himself waging a quiet war to stand up for what had been so good in the past. His attacks took various forms. When he found a wayward arrow, rather than return it, he'd snap it and slip it under one of his needle piles. Just this year, he's mustered the courage to sneak into Miss Caroline's office while she was with the girls watching one of their "fairy-tale-type movies" and slip into his pocket a pre-registration form a parent had sent in for the coming week. When the form couldn't be found on check-in Sunday, Miss Caroline would get all flustered at the impatience of the parent.

His sorties into the enjoyment of camp life were far too insignificant for Miss Caroline to notice at first, but the girls were much more perceptive. Jerry's condescending smiles were seen for what they were and the girls fought back with quiet mockings behind his back. One of their favorite tricks was for an entire group of twelve girls to follow behind him exaggeratedly shuffling on the insides of their shoes as Jerry did because of his flat feet. Fortunately for Jerry, he never attended Friday's amateur-night. One group was bound to come up with a comical portrayal of a portly man, huffing and puffing in an awkward waltz as he scraped pine needles along the ground.

When Miss Caroline finally understood the cruelty of the girls, she scolded them and charitably went to inform Jerry. But each time she approached him, his condescending smile was more than she could stomach and she found herself forcing a smile and then moving away. Unfortunately Jerry wished someone would stop him from playing his hopeless and painful war games.

WEDNESDAY IN THE THIRD WEEK OF LENT
Deuteronomy 4:1, 5-9
Matthew 5:17-19

Jesus, don't let me take You for granted. Don't let me put You on the outside of what's happening in my life. That isn't where You want to be. You are excited about everything that happens to me. You just don't want to sit back and not be involved. Today You speak to me about laws and regulations I have to perform to show my love for You. Thank You for giving me this direction. Thank You for caring enough to want me to grow through Your laws. Use Your power and strength to help me obey Your laws of love.

An Angry Christian?

I'm a terrible high school teacher; but I say this not without a good bit of experience. Right after Ordination, I was assigned to teach in a high school in the ghetto of Watts. I was delighted. The vitality and struggle for freedom I associated with the Black community were signs I knew of the presence of the Holy Spirit. I wanted to be a part of the action and offer what assistance I could. With all the idealism and enthusiasm I could muster, I went into the fray.

Sad to say, after not too long, I knew that I didn't have what it takes to do what I so wished I could. After two years I threw in the towel.

Do you know what my problem was? It wasn't that I didn't know my subjects well. My difficulty was that I had a terribly distorted image of Jesus.

I don't know where I picked up my confusion. I suppose there were many factors. I was brought up with a lot of very poor art when it came to images of Jesus. You know what I mean, don't you? Jesus with the ruddy cheeks and the long flowing just-shampooed-and-set-hair. Jesus looked like someone who had spent all His life resting in a shaded room on a big, soft cushion. There certainly wasn't much strength there! Subconsciously I began to think that being a Christian meant being an overly nice person. Anger and even raising my voice were plain and simple sins. Jesus was always meek and humble, smiling and patient and really so one-sidedly sugary that I shudder to think how naive He was to me.

Oh, it wasn't only artists who were responsible for my image of Him. I encouraged any tid-bit of knowledge about Jesus that had to deal with His niceness. After all, I could get away with so much more if Jesus didn't really care what I did. He was so vacillating and nice, I would never have to worry.

Deep down, though, I knew something was wrong. I wanted very much to love Jesus, but who could be enthusiastic about my image of Him? My fellow teachers in Watts really taught me a lot about Jesus. Here were men, dedicated to the same Jesus that I was, afire with the same enthusiasm. But they had discipline. When a student was doing something that was hurting himself or the class, they didn't smile and gently shake their heads. They got angry. They let their voices be heard. They laid down the law in no uncertain terms. Sure, the students would grumble and complain and cast all kinds of aspersions on the teacher, usually behind his back, but the students moved. They started to grow.

I started to grow also in a new understanding of Jesus. He was concerned in a very enthusiastic way in my life. He wasn't sitting back and letting me hurt myself as I was doing with my students. He was laying down the law in my life and wanted me to shape up! I saw Jesus moving in a new strength and power in my life. When I would be hypocritical in my actions, He would come to me with the same anger He had toward the Scribes and Pharisees who were saying one thing and doing another. With all the force of His Jewish temper, He was calling me a whitened sepulcher and a brood of vipers. I failed to understand His law of love in my life. Again and again, He would come at me with the same frustrated feelings with which He came to His Apostles and say, "how long do I have to put up with you?"

Jesus is exciting! He wants to be right in the center of everything that we're concerned with. Although He wants our love to be based on a free response, He's right in there giving us direction and spurring us onto greater dimensions of love.

How much our lives will change when we realize the power and strength, love and emotional excitement Jesus offers us. We are not a beaten people. We are an army in full force with a leader Who not only is known for His tender compassion and concern but has the fiery strength to ignite our beings with enthusiastic action.

Perhaps Christianity has fared so poorly of late because we haven't realized the deep strength we have in our leader. He's the Man-God Whose love is a balance of compassion and fiery enthusiasm. If we can convey this balance in our lives, perhaps Jesus will make more of an impact on the world He died to save.

THURSDAY IN THE THIRD WEEK OF LENT
Jeremiah 7:23-28
Luke 11:14-23

Jesus, it's so important that I have the openness to really listen to You. You are continually bombarding me with Your loving direction. But I have such a hard time listening. Help me to learn how to listen to You by really concentrating on listening to others.

Who's Listening?

The scene is a kitchen. Mother is bent over the stove. She is very hot and very busy. Suddenly upon the scene comes Tammy, twenty years old and bursting with enthusiasm.

Tammy: Mom ... (no response). Mother, it's happened!
Mom: Sure has.
Tammy: How did you hear?
Mom: Hear? You can smell it!
Tammy: What are you talking about?
Mom: This roast. Trying to get the potatoes ready and the roast burned. Hand me that knife.
Tammy: Mom, you've got to listen!
Mom: The knife!
Tammy: Here. Listen will you?
Mom: Tammy, have a heart, will you? Can't it wait?
Tammy: I don't believe this!
Mom: Have a heart, will you?
Tammy: Of course.
Stella: (She is Tammy's younger sister. Her hair is in curlers). Oh, there you are. So help me, if you have taken it.
Tammy: It?
Stella: Where's my blouse? The blue one?
Tammy: Hi Stella. How are things?
Stella: Don't get cute.
Tammy: Sorry, that was an unfair question. Didn't mean

to catch you off guard.

Stella: Well?

Tammy: Well indeed!

Stella: Where's my blouse?

Tammy: Oh, that. I think mom's using it over here.

Stella: Mother, do you have my blouse?

Mom: What are you talking about?

Stella: My blouse!

Tammy: Check the pan.

Stella: Mother, what are you doing with ... there isn't any blouse.

Tammy: Did you check your laundry hamper? Didn't you put it in there yesterday?

Stella: I did not. ... Oh, did I? That's right. I forgot.

Mom: Tammy, don't just stand there. Can't you see I'm in the middle of beef surgery. Give me something so I don't burn my hand!

Tammy: Here. Hey you two, are you ready for this?

Mom: Are *You* ready for this? (holding a burnt roast).

Stella: Hey mom, there's something burning in here.

Mom: The roast, honey! Wake up!

Stella: What did you do, burn it?

Mom: No, actually it's a special sauce I bought today. It's called "Charcoal a la delight"!

Tammy: I don't know if you realize this, but today is perhaps the most important day in my life.
(Father walks in). Are you ready for this?

Father: I don't know. I don't like to eat my meat too rare!

Mom: Very funny.

Tammy: Before we get too far from the subject at hand ...

Father: Which is?

Stella: I think mom burned the beef.

Mom: Really is bad, Bill.

Father: Hey, that's OK.

Stella: (leaving) Hey, Tammy. Thank you for reminding me about the laundry. Hey, could I borrow your red sweater? That would go with white pants.

Tammy: Sure.

Father: Hey, beautiful. That you standing around with the glazed look in your eye? What's happening?

Tammy: What, with me? Oh not much. Life's the same, old, boring merry-go-round it has always been.

Father: That's no good for my girl. You need some excitement.

Tammy: I'll keep my eyes open!

Mom: Tammy! (as if she were in the other room).

Tammy: Here! (as if she were calling from the other room).

Mom: Don't shout! Where's your sister? Dinner's ready!

FRIDAY IN THE THIRD WEEK OF LENT
Hosea 14:2-10
Mark 12:28-34

Jesus, I want to give You everything that I have. I don't want to hold back. This isn't easy. I so want to hold onto the material things that take up so much of my interest. They really become the same as the idols that You were so vehement against in the Old Testament. Help me to give up the sinful habits of my life. Help me to be free to really love You with everything that I have!

Jesus, Help Me Give You Everything!

We truthfully don't have much problem when it comes to giving the Lord fifty percent of everything that we are. We believe the Lord is worth that much to us. We can even go so far as to say that we could untie the strings to seventy-five percent to eighty percent of self and give that to the Lord. There's a problem though. Even when we're doing well on the road to perfection, giving all is really difficult. I'm talking about the five percent we're always anxious to hold back.

How easy we find flaunting our Christianity. We want everyone to look up to us as the great example. But deep in our hearts we know that we're afraid to give Jesus everything. Like the man in the Gospel today, there are just some things that we're too insecure to let go of. And yet, we know giving Jesus everything is the answer. This is how we can draw closer and closer in love with Him. This is how we can lose ourselves in love and be able to proclaim with Paul that it's no longer I that live but Christ that lives in me.

Way back in the Old Testament, the Lord through Hosea was telling us to be careful that we don't let material things become our gods. How true that story is today. So many things in life can hold us back from full giving.

For example: how easily television can slip in and become the time-consuming idol of our lives. "How could we have ever lived without it?" Oh, and there are so many other things that tie up my time and interest. How I wish that I were free to give all to the Lord. Do you ever wonder how people in the Stone Age bush country of the Philippines can live without a radio, car, dishwasher, clothes washer and dryer, typewriters, air-conditioning, central-heating, telephones and clocks?

The important tension in our lives has to be making sure that all these things are things we use and not things that are using us. We can so easily fall into a kind of slavery and be led around by the nose by the things that we're supposed to be using.

The important task I have to do in my life is draw closer and closer in deep personal love to Jesus. He has to be the object of my adoration and love. When I find other things are getting in the way, I have to cut them off. This is the big goal in life.

Another interesting point in this tension to make sure we are giving everything to the Lord, is by examining our expression of love for the Lord. As a Catholic, I tend to have a lot of intellectual approaches to the Lord. My worship is quite controlled. This was clearly seen in my reluctance to reach out to the person next to me at Mass and give a greeting of peace. This was a little too physical for my understanding of how I relate to the Lord. When I stop and think about it, if I really want to give everything in my worship and dedication to the Lord, I have to be careful that I just don't say "I love You" with my head or my voice. Perhaps my hands and arms should be used in the expression of my love. Well, why not even my feet and my whole being!

All this is for a purpose! We're not just wasting our time. We have a reward. Not only Eternity with all the love and peace that it will entail, but also the promise of a life of deep and lasting joy right here in the middle of our lives. Thanks to our focusing on Jesus, we experience freedoms that open all possibilities for joy and growth. Each morning will be a challenge filled with deeper and deeper meaning, all based on an ever new love of Jesus Christ.

SATURDAY IN THE THIRD WEEK OF LENT
Hosea 6:1-6
Luke 18:9-14

Jesus, I'm such a slave of rote! So often I find myself doing things without really thinking what I'm doing. This is so bad, especially when it comes to my relationship with You in prayer and the Eucharist. Give me Your gift of freshness. Let the things that I've done so many times over and over again take on a new meaning and life. You can do that if You will because You are the epitome of new life and freshness.

Parable of the Third of a Second

There was once a college student who, like the majority of college students, had very little money. When he came to his school, he had a terrible time finding a place to stay. Everything cost too much. After three tiring days of searching, and three freezing nights of sleeping on the beach, he discovered a room that was dirt cheap, well within his means. Oddly enough, the room was furnished and had all kinds of nice conveniences: a stove, dishwasher, beautiful fireplace, and a fine king-sized bed. There was even a fantastic view of the ocean. But there was one frightening drawback. The room had a large bay window looking directly out onto the gigantic revolving beacon of the lighthouse in the harbor. Every four seconds the comfortable little room was lit up with a blinding illumination for a third of a second.

His lack of money prevented him from getting anything better, but at least he would be kept warm from the cool breezes that swept across the ocean. He decided to give it a try and rented the room for a week.

The first days were nerve-wracking. Concentration on his studies was next to impossible. Every four seconds the intrusion would set the room aglow for a third of a second. He tried hoisting a blanket over the window but the space was too large and the light too penetrating. Under his breath, he muttered curses at either the person who built such big windows or the inventor of lighthouses. He even tried maneuvering himself around the room blindfolded, but black and blue shins proved too painful and he was forced to bear with the blinding rhythm of light.

A type of personal challenge developed. Would the student be bettered by a mechanical menace? "No fool light is going to get the better of me!", and the student dug in for the battle.

At the end of the first week when the landlord came to see if he planned to stay longer, there was little hesitation in the mind of the student as he doled out fifty-three precious dollars, the rent for six months.

In the beginning, college chums would come over to visit. The stay was not for long and you couldn't help detecting an ever so slight twitch of their heads every four seconds.

But the student soon learned to live with the light. As a matter of fact, the repetition of the light was so regular and similar that he found himself forgetting the light was there. As the months passed, so too life went on a normal routine for the student: eating, studying, reading, and wonder of wonders, even sleeping with a brilliant illumination coming every four seconds.

But one day, trauma was to enter into the life of the innocent and challenging student. A mouse was the culprit. Going too deep into a piece of cheddar, he bit into a lighthouse wire. The power went off for just a second. The circuit breaker was quick to pick up the slack but not quick enough! There was a stutter of light. In the months the student had been in the room, every four seconds had its meaning with the burst of light. But now, even though he was sound asleep, he was shaken to his very bones. He bolted up from a sound sleep and yelled to the top of his voice: "come back here."

The poor student was never the same. Two days later, the landlord grew suspicious because of the boy's absence. As he turned the master key and peeped into the room, he saw the frozen student sitting motionless in bed, his life forever scarred by that dark third of a second.

What to do with the student became a problem. When friends came to try to move him, the solid grip he had on the bed spoke more strongly than any lack of sounds coming from his gaped mouth or unblinking eyes as they were riveted in the direction of the light.

The landlord decided to let him stay, since renting the room to anyone else might end in a similar disaster. Friends came at regular times with food to try and nourish the light-struck student. Soon, though, the trauma of that third of a second took its toll and the only food he wanted was the soothing regular repetition of the flashing light. As death came for the student, he longed in vain to have the light fill up the gaping hole left in his life when the light failed for that third of a second.

FOURTH WEEK
OF LENT

MONDAY IN THE FOURTH WEEK OF LENT
Isaiah 65:17-21
John 4:43-54

Jesus, the royal official in today's gospel embarrasses me with his faith in You. Through his example help me to grow in faith. Don't let me slip into continually seeing your wonders in my life as merely natural occurences.

An Example of Great Faith

There is much to learn from the royal official John tells us about in today's gospel. Let's look a little closer into this extraordinary man.

Being a royal official meant that he was a member of a very elite group. He was closely associated with King Herod. Once we are able to see his office and importance, we are filled with wonder that he should go out of his way to contact Jesus. And go out of his way he did. John tells us that Jesus was in Cana and our royal official was from Capernaum. That is a distance of twenty miles. Think of a town that is twenty miles from your home. How readily would you walk that distance? And who was Jesus compared to this official? What humility and what a swallowing of pride for this royal official to go out of his way to beg help from some carpented from Galilee.

I can't help reflecting on how much greater this man's faith in Jesus was than mine today. Here the official was swallowing his pride and coming to Jesus in broad daylight for help and look how reluctant I am to witness the power of Jesus even to fellow Christians!

The second important point about our royal official is that he refused to be discouraged. Here a high official travels a good twenty miles to ask help of someone completely below his class. And what does he get? A rebuke! "Unless you see signs and wonders, you do not believe!" This isn't the only time we see Jesus act in this seemingly cool way. Remember the Canaanite woman who was seeking to have an evil spirit driven from her daughter? To her pleading, "Help me, Lord!" Jesus comes back with, "It's not right to take the food of sons and daught-

ers and throw it to the dogs." Ouch! In each of these cases we
see that Jesus wants to make sure those seeking his help are
in earnest. The signs that He worked were not just for show as
so many of those around Him seemed to want. Jesus was looking
for sincere dedication. And our royal official stood up to the
challenge. He wouldn't give up but persisted in his plea. And
how easily I lose heart in my prayers when the desired results
I'm petitioning don't come as quickly as I would like or in the
way I had planned.

Also from this little piece of conversation there is a clear
insight into the sincerity of Jesus. A royal official, a man close
to the power of Herod comes to ask Jesus for help. If I had
been running the show, I'm sure that I would have jumped at
the chance to ingratiate myself with this man of influence. But
not Jesus. He cared about this man and his needs and not what
he could get out of him. Jesus was willing to run the risk of
challenging his motives.

The third interesting point about this royal official is that
he went back home in faith without Jesus coming with him.
How easy it would have been to come to the conclusion that
Jesus was just playing along with him and trying to put him off.
Not only does Jesus rebuke him but he won't come home with
him to cure his son in person. Such an example forces me to
ask if my faith in Jesus' words is vague, nebulous and wistful.
Take for example the impressive words in John 14, 12. "The
man who has faith in me liwl do the works I do, and greater
far than these." And again, when Jesus says, "Ask and you
will receive." Do I merely think that these words *may be true* or
do I believe they *must be true*? Our royal official left knowing
Jesus' words *must be true*!

The final point of interest to be learned from our royal
official is that he surrendered his whole life to Jesus after the
miracle. When we ask God to work the wonders of His power
in our life and He does, there is usually a temptation to attribute the change to the natural course of events or a quirk of
nature. It is so easy to become ungrateful and ignore the moving
presence of the Lord in our life. The royal official didn't do

this. When he saw that his son was cured, he attributed this to the power of Jesus. He didn't stop there but he and his whole house became believers. God is working all kinds of powerful wonders of His love in our life today. Again and again, we have to make sure that we don't detachedly sit back and watch what is going on and not respond with loving thanks and renewed dedication to God who cares for us so much. And the royal official's response with his whole house was probably much more difficult than any response I can give today. His livelihood was working with Herod whose values were very much opposed to those of Jesus. Imagine the laughter and criticism he had to put up with from his peers. When at the end of Jesus' life we find Herod curious to see Jesus perform some wonders, perhaps our faithful and courageous official was the one who was witnessing to Herod of the miracles Jesus had worked in his family.

Let's pray today for the four characteristics of the royal official. May our pride never hinder us from seeking help from Jesus. May we never be discouraged but persevere in prayer. May our faith in Jesus' words be unwavering. And may we surrender to Jesus in total dedication!

TUESDAY IN THE FOURTH WEEK OF LENT
Ezekiel 47:1-9, 12
John 5:1-3, 5-16

Jesus, don't let me forget about the strength that You can exert in my life. When I try and handle things with my feeble means, I'm bound to end up in frustration. You are the One Who can come into my life like the force of a mighty flood water. You can wipe out anything that's not founded on You and start me off again. Do this now, please. I want Your power in my life to be the springboard for everything that I do. Help me to be smart and go where the real power is—You!

God of Power

Do you ever get a feeling of frustration at how ineffective you are in life when it comes to dealing with yourself and others? Because of our pride, we're continually going to have the tension of wanting to handle things our way but again and again realizing we're not the source of solutions that really count.

Our situation is similar to the little company of soldiers that has moved into a terribly precarious position. They are pinned down at the end of a high wall of mountains. The enemy is pressing in on all sides. Casualties are mounting. There doesn't seem to be any hope. The only exit possibility is over the wall of mountain but, right in the middle of the way out, the enemy has positioned a big menacing bunker which is belching out all kinds of rockets and bullets. At the command post, things are looking very bleak. Word goes out that a volunteer is needed to destroy the bunker. Help is not readily given, for to charge the bunker would most certainly mean death. But then, when all seemed lost, a young green-behind-the-ears private throws back the flap of the command-tent and swaggers in with an awkward salute. He clicks his heels and says, "Sir, Private Manning here, sir, reporting to volunteer to knock out the bunker." The commander can't believe his eyes. He's so happy. He walks over to Private Manning, shakes his hand and says, "Son, you are a man of courage and bravery. Thanks to you the lives of all the men in the company are going to be saved. I can give you no other instructions than to go up there and give the enemy in the bunker everything that you have!" With a gallant smile and another awkward salute, Private Manning crisply turns and moves out of the tent with all the glow of a dream come true. To the cheers of the men, who have now heard of his bravery, he looks straight at the bunker a couple hundred yards up the hill and moves out with a determined trot. There isn't even a thought of waving to his cheering comrades.

Half way up the hill the bunker starts firing its deadly rounds. There's a calm smile on Private Manning's face. He knows that the time for the kill has come. Suavely he reaches into his holster for his weapon. And what is it? A 45-caliber pistol. From behind a small rock, he takes a steady bead on the bunker and fires. Well, I know this is rather anti-climactic but you know as well as I do what happened. The puny 45-caliber bullets meant nothing to the big steel bunker. All the bravery and good will of Private Manning was for nothing because he was stupid. He was trying to destroy a big bunker with the wrong kind of weapon. He was foolish! Much more power was needed if he was going to win the battle with this bunker.

How often do we, when we run into the bunkers of our life, play the fool and not attack with the real power? Jesus is the real weapon to destroy the difficulties that we encounter in life. He is more powerful than twenty hydrogen bombs. So often we run into the battles of life with measly and ineffectual power.

The readings today speak of the power of God. We see Him as a mighty river moving with strength. The verse reminds us that a mighty God is with us. And then, wonder of wonders, look at the mighty power of Jesus today as he cures a man who had been a cripple for thirty-eight years. Imagine! Thirty-eight years. In walks Jesus and we see the mighty move of power. The same power can move in your life and mine against the bunkers of lack of communication, inability to understand oneself and inability to understand others, and enslaving habits. Let's be people who are smart in battle. Let's move with the power for victory. Let's make Jesus the center of our life. Let's allow the power of His Spirit to be a devastating flood destroying the opposition to our peace and union with the Ground of our Being.

Frustration and meaninglessness do not have to be a necessary ingredient of life. We are being called to victories by Jesus. Let's do it. We can. Jesus is waiting to give us what we need. He loves us. He died to prove it and longs that the power of His shed blood be not unused in our lives. All we have to do is call on Him. He will be there to help and lead us to the ultimate victory of Eternity with Him!

WEDNESDAY IN THE FOURTH WEEK OF LENT
Isaiah 49:8-15
John 5:17-30

Jesus, You know how I want to be free. I'm really spoiled. When too many people start to tell me what they want me to do, I have a hard time with that. I don't like restrictions. I don't like people telling me what I can and can't do. This is dangerous, Lord. When I reflect how You were subjected to the will of Your Father, I know I must follow on the same road of subjection if I want to really be free as You were. Help me to find my freedom, not in doing whatever I want but rather in subjecting myself to Your will. That's freedom!

Freedom Means Belonging!

Pippin is a musical with all kinds of plus's to it. The music is catchy. The lyrics are profound. The choreography, in the production on Broadway, was full of fun and precision. But the theme brought home in the final moments of the play was what made the strongest impression on me.

Pippin is the son of the Emperor Charlemagne. As the play starts, he's returning from Italy where he has just finished his studies. He is now ready to start life. He begins a quest to find his corner of the sky. He tries his hand at everything: the glory of a leader in battle, chasing women, taking over his father's job as King, and even becoming a religious leader. Nothing satisfies him. He even contemplates burning himself alive to let his existence go out in one final blaze of glory. That won't work. Everything is too confining. He wants to be free in his corner of the sky. Finally, in a beautifully staged conclusion, all the lights in the theater are turned out save for a solitary 100-watt bulb at center stage. Next to it stands Pippin and the widow he's afraid to commit himself to. In the heroic quest to find his corner of the sky and still remain free, he has come to the conclusion you can't be free unless you are tied to something. In his simple commitment to the woman he loves, he finds the basic meaning of freedom.

The idea really jolted me. How true but how hard to come by! If I want to be free, freedom can be found in no place aside from belonging to another. That seems to so go against the grain! I think my natural inclinations were similar to the answer some teen-ager gave me when I asked for a definition of freedom. "Hey man, when you're free, you do what *you* want. And you don't have to do what anybody else wants!"

As a Christian, this can't be the answer. Jesus gave me the key to the real meaning of freedom by His subjection to the will of His Father. I too must follow Christ in this regard and find my freedom in following the direction His commandments of love lead. This is how I can be free—really free.

Many Christians are struggling with the subject of divorce. My heart is really saddened by the word that in California, three out of five marriages end in divorce. Things come home even more when you think that recently there were more divorces than marriages in the county where I live. Frightening! I can't help feeling that somewhere at the base of this there is a great misunderstanding of the great ideals of freedom and happiness. Marriage isn't the only way of life that's affected by the confusion of the meaning of true freedom. I'm continually having to remind myself of Christ's understanding of freedom as I try to grow in my commitment to the religious vows.

How strange to my modern way of thinking to understand that a Trappist monk with walls to hem him in and all kinds of vows and regulations can have a freedom and happiness far beyond the most "liberated" playboy.

Jesus and His subjection has to be the ideal of my life in my struggle to be really free!

There is a profound and lasting result when I'm willing to allow my freedom to include subjection to the will of Jesus. As I commit myself to Him, He commits Himself to me and I come to the realization at the depth of my being that He loves me. He knows me for who I am, with my good points and weaknesses. He knows when I stand, when I sit, and He loves me. This is the key to my freedom, the greatest freedom possible. Jesus loves me just as I am, and now, with the backing of this love, there isn't anything I can't do. The sky is the limit. I am no longer enslaved by the fear of what other people might think about me negatively. I no longer have to live out the guilt of the evil I've done in my past life. I now have the freedom to dream of all the great things I can do with the gifts the Lord has given me and I can put them into actuality! Thanks to the deep personal love of Jesus for me, I know I have the backing of the greatest power and strength there is. He has created everything in existence. He is sustaining everything that's in my life. And He loves me. He accepts me and commits Himself to me. With that love, there is no limit to my freedom.

Let's re-new ourselves in subjection to Jesus. He will strengthen our awareness of His deep love for us, and, with that power and backing, we can strike out with a freedom that will make any freedom we've groped at before seem insignificant.

THURSDAY IN THE FOURTH WEEK OF LENT
Exodus 32:7-14
John 5:31-47

Jesus, I have to be careful when I pray. Sometimes I can get some pretty distorted images of just who You are. You can become so "other" that I lose touch with Your strong driving love to be a real person to me. Help me not to let You become other than God who has become man in order to share my life in all its ups and downs with the intimacy that Your almighty power has. Help me to pray to You as a friend who is open and concerned to hear what I have to say.

God Really Listens!

Have you ever sat down and tried to explain to yourself just how you would describe God in twenty words or less? This might really be an eye-opener. Now I don't necessarily mean a brief quiz on the Apostle's Creed. I'm talking about something extremely personal and honest.

In the past I've had several images of God and they all now make up who He is to me. One of my descriptions of God is that He is a law-giver. In the Church a great deal of stress was put on making sure that you obeyed the laws of God and of the Church. It wasn't too difficult to put too much stress on this aspect of our love relationship with God. It's easy to slip into thinking of an image of God similar to a judge down at the court-house, one who is very carefully watching to see if we've done wrong and then ready to dole out a sentence.

Later as I began reading through the Old Testament, I came across a God who was quite a warrior. I saw Him cheering on the Israelites as they destroyed enemy villages. God is not someone to fool around with. It's very important that you get on His side if you want to be free of tragedy.

Then I was introduced to the writings of Elie Wiesel and his accounts of the concentration camps during the second World War. Wiesel is a Jew who was one of the few fortunate

ones that made it through alive. This was a big part of my
quest to know God. A gnawing question came up again and
again. How could a God of love allow six million of his chosen
people to undergo liquidation? I learned that God loved freedom
and that freedom went to the extent of allowing His creation
to perpetrate such terrible deeds.

Today's first reading brings out an aspect of God that has
become very important to me, especially, in my prayer life with
Jesus. How do you sincerely and ultimately communicate with
an all-knowing God?

When I was small, I got a good dose of the fact that God is
eternal and all-knowing. The superlatives left me with the awe
and wonder of God that was intended. The awe and wonder
had the unfortunate factor of making God someone who was
a little too magnificent to be a real, tender lover of me and
my petty concerns and weaknesses. God became the "other."
One of my biggest difficulties was reconciling a God who was
all-knowing with the fact that He wanted me to come to Him
in prayer with my requests. If God is all-knowing, He very
easily can become a gigantic programed computer. For all
eternity, my program has been punched and He is just watching
as I go the way He has determined. As for prayer, He has programed that in. There are set times when I'll turn to Him
in prayer and He will "listen" and things will turn out all right.

Prayer under these conditions became necessary but a terribly
heartless thing. I really struggled with the notion of an all-
knowing God and the fact of Moses bargaining with the Lord
in today's reading. Or how explain Jesus saying that whatever
we asked the Father in His name, He would give us? And why
did Jesus urge us to pray the Our Father when all the while
He knew the outcome? How could Jesus act this way with me
when He was so vehemently angry with the Scribes and Pharisees
for their heartless dealings with people on such an impersonal
level?

Putting too much stress on God's "All-Knowing" attribute
makes Him terribly boring! I want God full of excitement.

I want God to really listen. I don't want God to be like the people who so infuriate me: when we discuss something they've made up their minds and are just going through the formalities of listening. I think God listens to me with love and special attention. Although He's all-knowing, He's also powerful enough to break out of my petty categories of logic, and, along with being all-knowing, He is willing to change the course of events of the future because of my feeble, confused, but sincere prayer.

My ideal is to have the intimacy of Moses in conversing with the Lord and to know, although He knows everything, He's also anxiously listening. He's freshly open to me every time I turn to Him.

FRIDAY IN THE FOURTH WEEK OF LENT
Wisdom 2:1, 12-22
John 7:1-2, 10:25-30

Jesus, sometimes my dreams have a habit of just not coming true. I try to reach out and effect the things I think I should, and many times things just fall through. When I experience failure in life, help me to know that I'm not alone. You too knew the heartbreak of failure. You were turned away by the very people that You loved. Thank You for doing that. You help me and give me strength. Please continue to be my strength.

Jesus' Failure

If you are a person who tries to do something with your life and are willing to risk your love and enthusiasm by giving them to people, you are going to experience failure. We don't like that word because it seems a disgrace. But, if we are giving persons, failure, nine times out of ten, is going to be an integral part of our lives. The pity is many people, after they reach out and experience failure, stop reaching out.

Because we are people who dream and want to put those dreams into actuality, failure is a possibility—a probability. A woman dreams of being a mother. She wants her dream-man to come along but nothing seems to happen. Failure is a long gnawing experience for this thirty-five-year-old woman who has never been able to find a husband. Or again, in our idealism, we set out to tackle a job. Full of enthusiasm, we move into a ghetto neighborhood to teach school. Soon we know that good will and enthusiasm just aren't enough. There's a gift to teaching, and as of now it hasn't been developed in us. We experience the failure of our ideals.

Failure doesn't have to be associated with such momentous things such as finding a partner for life or discovering a career. Failure can occur, perhaps in a more hurting way, in our simple inability to communicate ourselves to the people with whom we live.

We must be careful we don't just sweep the facts of our

failure under the rug or hide them in the closet when people come by. Failure can be very positive, for it can give us a good knowledge of who we are. We understand better where our strengths and weaknesses are. Failure is good too because it can deepen our relationship with Jesus.

Did you ever think of Jesus as experiencing failure? He did, you know, in many ways. He had a tireless hunger for truth and love. This love reached out to His close friends, the people He was brought up with, and His own race, the Jews. In His struggle to bring the truth and love of God's kingdom in a personal way, He was met with so much misunderstanding. Although this was not what He aimed for, the friends and all Jews thought Jesus was trying to be a temporal ruler. Again and again we see Him trying to set people straight. But His miracles, His love for sinners, His parables, His anger, and His fulfillment of scriptures were all misunderstood. As He is about to die, we see Him crying over Jerusalem. He so wanted things to be different than they were. He had aimed for something, something full of truth and love, and where was it going to get Him? They were going to throw Him outside the city He loved and nail Him to a tree.

As long as our striving is for truth, motivated by love after the example of Jesus, the failures we'll experience will have a difference. Sure they'll hurt, even may border on being devastating, but there is hope! There is a strength even in the midst of the worst scene of falling flat on your face.

Jesus, who is our life and has drawn us to Himself, has died and come to life. He has shown a power that is the greatest strength the world has ever heard of. And that strength and power loves me. And that love understands me. Jesus knows, first hand, the sorrow of my life. He won't abandon me. He is beside me with a hope that will never end. In His power and love, as I wonder in the sorrow of my shattered dreams, Jesus takes my hand and promises me His love for all eternity. The failure of a Christian is always bright with hope.

SATURDAY IN THE FOURTH WEEK OF LENT
Jeremiah 11:18-20
John 7:40-53

Jesus, often I find that when people refer to You as the Lamb of God, I cringe. You were so full of love for the people who put You to death. Just like a lamb who is being led to the slaughter, You didn't open Your mouth. When people don't treat me the way I think I should be treated, do they ever hear about it, and also everyone within shouting range. Give me Your love so that I can bear with difficulties. Give me patience. Help me to act as You did in Your life and accept the death of my pride and puffed-up image of myself with a closed mouth.

Dying without Squeals

The title of Christ, the Lamb of God, has always had a special significance for me because my father was a meat-packer. One evening, at home, he fascinated me with the story of how animals were slaughtered down in the yards of Chicago where he had worked. Back when he was in the business, the slaughter of cows was rather brutal. They were lined up in a narrow aisle and then prodded up an incline. The din they made was terrible. The smell of death could be picked up by them for blocks. As they came to the end of the corridor, a strong man would come out yielding a big club and knock the cow several times over the head into senselessness. Thank goodness things are more humane now. It was worse for pigs! They would be led down a similar corridor, subjected to the same prodding, but the piercing noise they made was ten times more frightening. As pigs came up the steep incline, they were in a frenzy because of the smell of blood from those that went before them. The slaughter took place, not with a club but with a large butcher knife. (By this time in the story, my color had quite paled and I was frantically gulping to offset the lightness of my head.) But with lambs, the scene was entirely different. Sure, there was the same corridor and incline and smell of blood, but there was no prodding and there was no noise. The lamb would stand patiently in line for its turn and when it came the lamb would be smoothly slit across the throat and drop.

I often tell that story at Mass. The nearest we come to knowing about the slaughter of a lamb is the neatly packed piece of mutton in the grocer's cooler.

Jesus is the Lamb of God! Jeremiah says He was led to the slaughter like a lamb. We need to reflect on this difficult aspect of the life and death of our Leader, for we who have given ourselves to Him must follow in His footsteps. The many deaths we experience in our life of coming closer and closer to Jesus must be in the mold of Jesus' death.

One of the most difficult deaths I experience as a Christian is having to go to confession. It kills me! I have to drop that transparent mask I'm flaunting and tell another person, who knows me, that I'm a sinner! I'm afraid I don't go out in this death like the quiet lamb. I'm full of all kinds of noise—noise in the form of explanations and rationalizations and trying not to make things look so bad. I need to imitate Jesus in His death and be quiet. All I have to do is state the truth in all honesty and simplicity.

Another death I undergo as a Christian is being of service. I find this especially hard when I've planned how I would like my day to go today. I'm going to get around to doing those things I've been putting off for such a long time. Finally I'll get to them. And then what happens? The phone rings and someone needs me and I have to throw up for grabs all my well-made plans. Again, this death-to-myself experience usually isn't close to the quiet lamb-like death of Jesus. I do more hemming and hawing before I 'whole-heartedly' condescend to change my precious plans and help someone.

Another sharing I have with the death of Jesus is the death I undergo to move out of my hectic and noisy day and be quiet in prayer. You would think I was having to undergo a gigantic hypodermic needle the way I sidle away from sitting in Chapel and being quiet for half an hour. The racket I make! Not externally but inside. I take so long to settle down and be quiet. With radio, TV and phones and what-not, being quiet is a killer.

We all have to die several times each day. If you get a chance, think about the many times you encounter death to yourself. Think of the Lamb of God and the terrible injustice He underwent, all with the patience and love that has to be the way of our deaths. Ah, but for the Christian, these deaths are fraught with so much hope. We know that from these deaths we will arise to a new life of deeper love for Jesus and a greater ability to embrace death continually throughout our life like the true Lamb of God.

FIFTH WEEK
OF LENT

Jesus, as a child of this modern age, I'm really influenced by
television. At times, I wonder how I ever got along without it!
There's much that's good on the tube but there's also a great
deal that frightens me. In a very subtle way my values are
being influenced. It is so easy for me to think that if they say
things on TV it must be the way things are. Help me not to
go along with the crowd. Help me to make my own decisions
about what's good and what's bad. Help me to be more choosy
in what I watch!

Television for Jesus

Today's story about Susanna is fascinating. I'm sure there must
be some TV writer in Hollywood who's frantically searching
for a story-line for an episode for next season's "who-done-it"
series. If he hears today's reading from Daniel he has it!

Look at the ingredients of that story: two nasty old men
who are villains of the first class, and a beautiful young house-
wife who is the epitome of goodness and innocence. There is
even a sinister case of blackmail and a courtroom scene of
high tension. The perfect attorney-at-law, who, by his cunning,
comes in and foils the wicked designs of the enemy and brings
justice. The ending is happy! I defy you to change the channel
with a plot like that!

With this intriguing story as a starting-point, let's examine
TV's influence in our lives as Christians.

Television is here to stay. I've heard various statistics but
they all center around the ridiculous time of three hours a day
the average American spends before the television. This isn't
so bad itself. What frightens me is that the influence can be
so strong and subtle. While we are reflecting this Lent how
we can grow into a deeper relationship with Christ, we should
look closely into this media to see if it's helping or hindering.
We have to be careful we don't just move along with everyone

else and think that if the TV says so, this must be the accepted way of doing things. This is the big danger of the mass media and also the gigantic strength. What one person can say in a small studio in downtown Burbank can easily be considered the norm of action for millions of people. (A TV executive once mentioned to me that if a national series has only a regular audience of 14,000,000 people it's bound to be cancelled for the next season.)

I find the TV media conveying strong ideas about two very important things: sex and materialism. As a follower of Jesus, I have to continually make sure the teachings of Jesus on these matters are not contradicted by what I'm being taught on TV.

Infidelity in marriage and pre-marital sex are not things that shock me anymore on TV. They are natural courses of action that any red-blooded person does with a minimum of remorse. As a follower of Jesus, my values are contrary to these actions. Unless I make a conscious effort to uphold what I believe, the TV will water-down how different I'm supposed to be than the rest of the world.

Are you as amazed as I am at the large amounts of money given away on the game shows? I'm frightened by the conclusion that a lot of money is what happiness is all about. The more I watch these people winning money, the more I wish that I had money. Very subtly, the ideal of my life is centered around money and merchandise. I have a hard time reconciling the money interest on the game shows with the poverty and simplicity that Jesus lived.

I'm not advocating running away from TV. Far from it! Television is a powerful vehicle to bring across the good news of Jesus. I'm not advocating a defensive action but rather an offensive one. I'm convinced through the personal love of Jesus we should start to use all our efforts to flood the media with the truth of Christ. Christ is the answer to man's tireless search for happiness. Each and everyone of us should pray for direction and then be open in following the Spirit into effective use of the media. We might offer our talents professionally or we might offer financial aid as best we can to foster the kingdom's coming in our day through the television.

As we foster a deeper and deeper love for Jesus, we'll find ourselves wanting to express this love to as many people as we can. Television is a fine means.

TUESDAY IN THE FIFTH WEEK OF LENT
Numbers 21:4-9
John 8:21-30

Jesus, I want to thank You for coming into this world two thousand years ago. I thank You again for not leaving me after Your Ascension but for coming and living with me today. Help me to realize Your presence in my life. Don't let me think of You as someone who lived long ago or far away. You are now, Jesus. Become the sign in my life that gives me direction. Show me, in Your loving way, what You want me to do in my life. Help me to see You raised up today in Your Mystical Body.

By What Sign?

My work as a priest is a Vocation Director. I spend most of my waking hours dealing with young men who are struggling with the decision to become missionary priests and brothers. I love this work. I know that in the selfless dedication of men and women to Jesus, we have the key to ushering in the kingdom of God in our day.

I try as best I can to help people make the best decision for Christ. The question comes up again and again, "How can I know the Lord is calling me to this or to that?" These gnawing questions are not just concerned with the priesthood or the religious life. What about knowing if I should marry this person? Should I commit the rest of my life to a person I'm not sure that I know? Or what about changing a job or moving into another life style?

Since we are human, we start to look for signs. We look for some kind of a thermometer that will tell us what seems so intangible.

There are all kinds of signs that we employ to help give us direction. Shakespeare tells of Caesar looking to the entrails of animals for direction to the future. There are very few papers that don't carry a daily astrological chart to help you with what you should or shouldn't do today. (I always have to smile

when I see those charts because I was born in the end of December, the same sign as Jesus!) Gypsies are known for reading
tea leaves and palms. And come election time, the great com-
puterized polls we have can predict the election's results within
one or two percentage points.

Today's Psalm verse speaks of what we often feel in the
loneliness of making a decision of importance. The Lord seems
to hide His face from us. We long for Him to show the way.

In our struggle to discern the correct sign for making a
decision, today's Gospel is quite simple in its solution: Jesus
lifted up on the cross is our sign!

Now what does that mean practically? I think this directs
us to three courses of action. The primary thing that we
must do is put the quandary in the hands of the Lord in prayer.
We must be extremely simple and honest in asking Him to
solve our dilemma. Sometimes this prayer should be joined
with fasting and a greater rein on the evil habits we are in-
clined to. The second step is reading and meditation on Jesus
in the Scriptures. After praying for insight from the Holy Spirit,
we must open Scripture on a regular daily basis and really
listen to the Word of God. Finally, we must consult the Body
of Christ. This can mean several things: talking with a person
we trust as being close to Jesus, reading documents of the
Church, reading spiritual writings and in general, being attentive
to the whole world in which we live.

One of the dangers of being too specific in describing how
the Lord will be a sign to us is that we box-in the Lord. Jesus
can speak to us in unexpected ways. We might see His direction
as clearly as day after seeing a good movie or play. We might
be listening to the radio and a hard rock band will come
pounding at our eardrums with the simple solution. We might
even fall off a horse and break a leg and have the solution
right there.

I don't think the decisions we make with the Lord have
to be accompanied by ulcers and nervous breakdowns. When
we turn to the Lord, we're turning to a great power. He has

control of things and wants us to relax in His love. This is an important sign of His presence in our decisions—peace and truth.

How much more sense putting my trust in Jesus makes rather than in astrology, tea-leaves or computers. Jesus is the Creator and Sustainer of everything that's in existence.

WEDNESDAY IN THE FIFTH WEEK OF LENT
Daniel 3:14-20, 91-92, 95
John 8:31-42

Jesus, I pride myself on being really free. But the more I talk this matter over with You, I know that I have a long way to go before I'll be as free as You want me to be. Help me confront the prejudice and revenge and hedonism that so subtly is controlling my life. Free me from all sin.

Those Not-So-Conscious Sins!

The Jews in the time of Jesus were a very proud people. They gloried in the fact that they were not slaves to anyone or anything. Even though the Romans were occupying their country, they maintained a fierce independence and freedom. Knowing this strong pride, we can understand why they reacted so strongly to Jesus' statement, "If you live according to my teachings . . . you will know the truth and the truth will set you free." We can almost feel the earth quake with their response, "Never have we been slaves to anyone!"

We, like the Jews of 2,000 years ago, are also very proud of our freedom. We have fought a war to gain independence from England. How many lost their lives in the Civil War over the issue of Negro slavery? We fought two wars to maintain freedom in Europe. We dropped an atomic bomb to make sure that the Pacific could live in freedom. And twice we have fought to allow the people in small countries in Asia the right to self-determination. To say that we are not free is almost an affront to the lives that were given to maintain freedom here and around the world.

And yet, even though Jesus knows the extent that we have gone to maintain freedom, He says to us today as He did to the Jews two centuries ago, "Despite all the wars and riots and legislation and marches you are slaves. And only if you start living my words will you ever be free!"

The slavery that Jesus speaks about of course is the slavery to sin.

Like the Jews we are angry that our freedom is questioned. But this anger is understandable since often we don't experience this slavery on a conscious level. Many times our actions are dictated by values that were instilled in us by our parents and those influencing us as children. As we grew up, we needed direction. We were like a tape recording machine that was turned on at birth and filled up with all kinds of values from other people: "People with skin of a different color don't make good neighbors." "Sex is a dirty word." "People with good manners rise when a lady enters the room." "God is an old man sitting on a cloudlike throne with a long flowing beard." "When someone does you wrong, get back at them."

As we move through life, often we are unconscious slaves to these values that have been put on our tape-recorder. When a person of a different race moves in next door, we have been so conditioned and enslaved by the values others have put on our tape-recorder, we simply play back our learned response and, not maliciously, move away.

Until we examine our values and start acting out of personal conviction, we are slaves to the beliefs of others.

Sin's enslavement is not always as subtle as doing things because others have told us. Many times we are slaves to pleasure. We are very much like children who live on a very natural plane. If a horse pill is going to be distasteful and painful going down, children will run away even though the horse pill will be the only remedy for a terrible stomach-ache. Children live on a natural plane. Anything that gives pleasure is good. Anything involving pain is bad. And so choices are made to play baseball rather than practice the piano. Many of our adult sins are reflections of this childish slavery to pleasure. Adultery is chosen because it feels good even though one's family may be ruined. I let my temper go unchecked even though I am wiping away the glow of hope from the eyes of my husband and children.

True freedom will come when I refuse to live on a pleasure/pain basis. Certainly I don't reject pleasure when I follow Christ.

But immature gratification is not to be the dominating factor in my choices of life.

Jesus has come to bring us the freedom of His truth. With His guidance, we will stop doing things blindly or because "They've always been done that way." As many actions as possible will be done out of the struggle of personal conviction. The happiness involved with real freedom will be seen to include the pain of being concerned for another's good.

This is the most important war for freedom we can wage. And perhaps if more and more of us could take up the fight, the more deadly wars with bullets and bombs wouldn't be necessary.

THURSDAY IN THE FIFTH WEEK OF LENT
Genesis 17:3-9
John 8:51-59

Jesus, so many times I've fallen short of the dream I have deep in my heart for myself. At times I get discouraged by this. Then I start to think of Your love for me and I get new courage. You really like me. Even when I get down on myself You are there with Your support. I really thank You for committing Yourself to me and for promising me the wonder of wonders, everlasting life with You. You really are too good, but thank You so much anyway. Help me to live up to the trust You've put in me.

God Believes in Me

One summer, during grade school, I traveled from my home in Kentucky to visit relatives in the big city of Chicago. The big city life was quite a thrill. One part of that trip I'll never forget was going to Soldier Field for the Fourth of July fireworks. I had never seen anything like that. The part that was so important to me, though, was at the half-time of the show. After being dazzled by all the fireworks for an hour, a man walked to the center of the field. There must have been 100,000 people there, or so it seemed to me. He said that he was going to do something quite impressive. I squirmed to get a better view around the person sitting in front of me. The man on the field asked everyone in the stadium to put out any cigarettes. Then he said he was going to turn out the gigantic floodlights that ringed the stadium. Suddenly, the lights which had given the impression of daylight were extinguished and all the thousands of people were in complete darkness. After a sound of "ah" at the magnificence of the darkness, there was a moment of quiet. The experience of those few moments etched itself into my memory and I used the experience as an example many times. Then out of the midst of that darkness, the man in the middle of the field spoke. He asked us to direct our attention to the middle of the field where he was. Then, quite simply, he lit a match. Another sigh of wonder was heard from the thousands of people. There in the midst of that total darkness a light shone and it gave direction and warmth to so many.

Have you ever stopped to think what death was like before Jesus? What would life be like without the promise of everlasting life? I couldn't help comparing the experience of the total darkness of Soldier Field to the gnawing frustration and fear people would have experienced in the face of a death which was all that there was! Even now, death is such an unknown and feared thing. I think of all the pills that are taken, the airplanes that aren't flown, the seat-belts that are surely fastened, the regular check-ups that are taken, the fat that is jogged off, the fear of heights and, in general, the great care we take to insure a long life.

We have very strong instincts against death and we have strong fears because it is such an unknown and we fear the things we don't know. And now, in the midst of this fear, which comes so meaningfully when we share the death of a dear friend, Jesus walks with the greatest words of peace and joy that man could ever experience. "If you believe in Me, you will never die." How often we've heard this and yet it's so fundamentally strong and meaningful. Jesus has made a covenant to ward off the thing I fear most in life. He has reached out a hand of love to the most fretful thing I know. He has told me that I'll never die. Suddenly, in the midst of a soldier's field that is filled with darkness, a light appears and there is hope and there is warmth! Jesus has promised me Eternal Life.

I shake my head at the wonder of such a stupendous bargain. Who am I to receive this gift! How could He entrust this gift to me? Look at me! Look at my fickleness! Look at my rollercoaster constancy! And yet, Jesus says He believes in me. He thinks I'm worth the risk. He's willing to back me even though my credit is so very poor.

How much I need to deepen the thanks I give to the Lord Jesus for the love that He's given me. He loves me with all my sins and weaknesses. He knows me in and out. There is nothing that's hidden from Him. But He still likes me. He believes in me! Oh, if I could only let this sink into the marrow of my bones. He loves me! And from this I can move to love myself and then I can move to love others with a new-found freedom. Oh, Lord, help me to live up to the love You've committed to me!

FRIDAY IN THE FIFTH WEEK OF LENT
Jeremiah 20:10-13
John 10:31-42

Jesus, so much of my time is spent trying to prove to others that I am better than they are. I so want to be number one. But when I draw closer and closer to You, I see how much of a servant You were to the people You lived with. Your aim wasn't to show how You were better than others. You wanted to give Yourself to them. At times I'm frightened by that seeming weakness. Help me to know that You love me. With that strength, I can relax with myself and You.

When I'm Weak I'm Strong

Being Number One is so important to us. Whether it's us as a country, an organization, a family or an individual, we are very much concerned about not being Number Two. As a country, we spend a great deal of money and effort to have the best space program and the strongest military defense. I wonder how many business people develop ulcers each day in attempts to outsell the competition. Avis even makes a point of getting to Number One by advertising they're Number Two. You have to think about that for awhile! Sad to say, there's even this competition among Christians.

I'll never forget going to one of those Pee-Wee Tackle Football games. As I was munching on my hot-dog, waiting for the game to start, I looked over to my side and there behind the bleachers was a large man standing over his son. The little guy must have been all of three and a half feet. He was all dressed up for combat. His helmet was three sizes too big, for when he nodded to his father, the helmet moved in a definite bobbing motion around the head. The shoulder pads were quite over-sized for the boy's frame. The father was bent over the boy with both hands on the enlarged shoulders and was saying with all the gusto of a Knute Rockne: "All right, son, I want you to get out there and kill. None of this mamsy-pamsy stuff. I want you to win." And the helmet gently bobbed away as the child nervously nodded an unconvincing consent.

Again, I wonder how many marriages go on the rocks because of the competition that develops. How often I run into the problem of one partner being outraged because the other thinks that he or she has to dominate.

In the face of a world competing to be Number One, Jesus does a very uncomfortable thing. He gets down on His knees and washes the feet of His Disciples. What kind of strength is that? And then, although He's Almighty God, He allows the people He loves to crucify Him. That mode of life is really hard to get excited about when you're so concerned about being Number One. As if that weren't enough, Paul strengthens the point when he says, "when I'm weakest, that's when I'm strongest of all."

If we find ourselves being disheartened by this challenge, today's readings give us courage. The God Whose example we follow in our weakness and service is a God of mighty strength and complete control. As we read in Jeremiah, the Lord is a "mighty hero." We don't have to be afraid of following His example of service and weakness. The Lord will be all the strength that we need. He is a rock, a fortress and a deliverer. He shows His real power in the Gospel when a mob tries to arrest Him and He eludes them. Although He is a servant and appears to be weak, he has every situation completely under control.

The desire to continually be better than another is indicative of a lot of insecurity with ourself. Jesus confronts this problem with His love for us. The special attraction He has for us gives us confidence in ourselves. With His backing, we can stand on our own two feet and don't have to continually be looking back or down at people we deal with. Because of the powerful love of Jesus for us, we can relax. His love is all that really matters. We don't have to prove ourselves to others when we have such a magnificent love in Jesus.

To others the idea of service might be a frightening weakness but when founded on a deep personal love of Jesus, it's an enriching expression of love founded on strength.

SATURDAY IN THE FIFTH WEEK OF LENT
Ezekiel 37:21-28
John 11:45-57

Jesus, when I read about You in the Bible, I see You continually trying to bring people together. Unity was such a dominant theme in Your life. Sad to say, Your Mystical Body, the Church, has a great deal of division. Help me to do my part to bridge the separation. Help me to be sincerely concerned about listening and loving my brothers and sisters who are of other denominations. Help me not to be lording it over with them but rather listening and needing. Help Your love to be the motivation for my concern.

Needing Is the Key to Unity

So much of Jesus' life was spent bringing people together! Again and again, He would see people separated from others and He'd try to do something about unity! The blind men, the leper, the cripple, all were ostracized from society and His cure brought them back. They wanted to stone the woman caught in adultery and Jesus was concerned with bringing her back to becoming the person she should be. One of Jesus' signs of His ministry to John the Baptizer was preaching the good news to the poor. Formerly people without financial influence were rejected but Jesus was concerned with the separation and wanted to bring all into the kingdom. The Samaritans were despised by the Jews who worshiped in Jerusalem. Jesus worked wonders with Samaritans and even made one a hero of a parable. That probably infuriated Jews who wanted to keep the Samaritans in their place, but Jesus wanted them to come and be united in His Name. Just before His death, He makes very explicit His desire for unity in His high priestly prayer. Even today's Gospel has Caiphas proclaim that Jesus' death would gather into one all the dispersed children of God.

In our day, one of the most hurting disunities is the ugly rupture that's occurred between Christians. Fellow believers in Jesus don't talk to each other and nurture great feelings of con-

descension or kill each other. The number of Christian denominations who have little or nothing to do with each other is
abominable!

The deeper we grow in union with Jesus, the better we will
see how close unity was to His Heart. From this we should
experience a great restlessness and anger with anything that
frustrates the unity of Christians which is so diabolically opposed
to the Jesus we love. As we grow deeper and deeper in love
with Jesus, we will be put on fire with the Pentecostal Flame
of the Holy Spirit and want to be missionaries of the good
news. As we reach out, we'll be struck smack in the face with
the frightening obstacle of Christians who don't have anything
to do with each other. If they're not killing each other they're
condescendingly smiling at the ignorance of each other. Who
can be attracted to such disunity? We must come together on
a united front before we can really be effective in making Jesus
the vital influence He has to be in our lives and in the lives
of everyone in the world.

In our striving to bring about unity with fellow Christians,
we have to make sure we use our heads. One of the key words
to success in ecumenical efforts is "need." If I am going to be
influenced by anyone, it will be by someone who needs me.
If I feel, in talking to someone, that I have something to offer
to him and he's willing to take what I hold dear and sacred,
we're going to be able to get together. If, on the other hand,
the person I communicate with has already decided he has all
the possible answers and has no need of me, I'm going to
waste my time being hurt by having my love smashed against
a brick wall.

We must become very positive in our concern. What we
need, more than anything else, is deeper insights into knowing
and loving Jesus and this is what other denominations can
give. Each sincere denomination has tapped a beautiful well-
spring of Jesus in its isolation. Let's uncover the unity we
have in our common Savior Who was so strong in bringing
people together. I know there is a long hard struggle because

of our differences, but until the antagonism and indifferences are resolved Christianity is so very weakened.

Let's start! Prayer is the first step. Then, with the deepening relationship with Jesus, a restlessness with the division will come in. From this a sincere search for Jesus will help us to get away from this terrible division. The bridge to this unity we aim for is a sincere need and openness.

Could you imagine Christianity today without the denominational differences we have? What a strong sign of the coming of the kingdom. What a beautiful foretaste of what heaven will be like.

HOLY WEEK

MONDAY IN HOLY WEEK
Isaiah 42:1-7
John 12:1-11

Jesus, Holy Week begins. I want to try and be very close to You through the liturgy as together we relive the events of this week. Today I see Your apostles are very concerned that if You are to die, this will be a terrible waste of effective action. Why don't You keep side-stepping the people that are trying to kill You and keep doing the good work that You've done for so many years? Help me to understand why You were willing to allow death to come when there seemed to be so much more that could have been done.

Waste

As Jesus moved closer and closer to Good Friday, His death became more and more a probability. In today's Gospel, His Body was anointed for the day of His burial. Death was in the air. The anger and hatred of the Jewish leaders was reaching a pitch not heard before. Christ seemed to be moving down a dead-end street. This must have been very difficult for the apostles to believe.

Jesus was so full of love and miraculous power, His death would be too pointless a waste to even imagine. Jesus must have struggled with this too for He wanted to reach so many with His love and now His death would seem to leave things unfinished. Giving one's life away, just at this time, when so much more good was possible! What a waste!

But for Jesus, spending Himself, wasting if you will, was the only way of life He knew. His giving death was quite in line with His way of life. He didn't know how to preserve Himself. All he could do was give away.

Unchristian values call this foolish waste. As followers of Jesus, we must embrace this "foolish waste" as our natural mode of existence. This is very difficult, for society's values militate against "wasting" self.

For example, thanks to magazines, movies, TV commercials

and bill boards, we are instilled with the goal of the "ideal woman" and the "ideal man." The hair-style may vary, and cut of clothes may change. But, through it all, the attractive beauty queen image and the combination quarterback-lawyer image comes across loud and clear as the ideal of every normal man and woman. As age takes its toll, the battle to preserve these ideals is fought with cosmetics, diets, exercise, mild dish soap, wigs and elixirs.

One frightening obstacle in the pursuit of these ideals is the rearing of children. Today, I pick up such a great reluctance among couples to have children. There may be many legitimate reasons such as sanity or health or finances. But one reason that bothers me is the fear of losing the image of the ideal man and woman. What's bound to happen with one or several children will be that all the attractiveness we have will be wasted on the upbringing of children. This concern is really dangerous for a Christian. Wasting oneself in an act of love is what Christianity is all about. The gifts God has given us are not to be preserved for themselves but are to be wasted in the love of others.

The ideal of Christian beauty and attractiveness should take a different direction than the preservatives we are exposed to in the media. Our concentration must be that of Jesus Who was more concerned about giving Himself than preserving even His life.

As followers of Jesus, we must not be selfish but willing to use all our strength: physical, mental and emotional in the service of others. In this we will do what Jesus does. And a beautiful person will emerge.

Grey hair will develop from patiently dealing with a confused teenager. Wrinkles of concern will line our face over an ailing parent. Muscles will be used up from carrying the burdens of others. Hearts will grow weaker through continually running after someone who's lost. And bags will develop under eyes that stay awake too many times to care for a sick child or a friend who just had to have someone to talk to. Pretty soon, all this expense of self will take its toll in death as with Jesus. But what lies ahead is an eternity of beauty, freshness, joy and unrestricted love.

TUESDAY IN HOLY WEEK
Isaiah 49:1-6
John 13:21-33, 36-38

Jesus, today in the liturgy You are deeply troubled. You have
spent Your whole life giving Yourself in love to Your Apostles
and Your people and now when the chips are down there seems
to be so little of Your love being returned. You are really
struggling with a deep and hurting loneliness. I must be sensitive to this in my life right now. I must strive to return Your
love and not fall into the fault of my brothers, the Apostles,
and leave You or fail to return Your love. Help me, Jesus,
to be constant in my faithfulness to You.

Loneliness

A few years ago, a plane full of rugby players was flying over
snow-covered mountains in South America. There was a mis-
calculation by the pilot and the plane went crashing into the
snowy mountains. Many people were killed but, fortunately,
there were several people who survived. Although there were
many injured among the living, there was a great deal of hope
that they would be rescued. There was a problem, though.
Since the pilot had gone way off course, the search planes
that were sent out didn't concentrate on the area of the crash.
What ensued were frightening months for the survivors in their
attempt to live.

More difficult than the pain of their injuries, the hunger
in their stomachs and the slow deaths of friends, was the
frightening realization that they were alone. After the first few
weeks, they knew that those in charge of rescue had given up
thinking about survivors. The rescuers would wait until the
spring thaw to find the wreckage and return the bodies for
burial. The terrain was such that escape seemed impossible.
The frequent snow storms made travel a dim possibility. The
frightening experience of being alone lasted for several months.
Many of the living simply gave up hope in this terrible experience of loneliness. A handful hung on for the long months,

eating the dried flesh of dead comrades. Eventually, some were able to escape the walls of snow and find help.

We all have experienced the anguish of being alone at one time or another. Perhaps it was that first day in school when the parents we always depended on were suddenly gone. Perhaps a long relationship had to be broken and, with quick harshness, a regular support in our life was gone. Perhaps a friend or marriage partner died and we were forced to go it alone.

As His life reaches its turning point, Jesus is deeply hurt by the loneliness of knowing His Disciples were about to flee Him. Jesus spent His whole life making investments of love in the people He met. As Paul says, He was continually pouring Himself out, emptying Himself in an act of love for His friends. As death became more and more of a reality, Jesus must have reflected on the seeming futility of entrusting so much of Himself to others when they would go so far as to deny that they knew Him. He had so reached out to others. He shared His joy and sorrow, His tiredness, His exuberance and His frustrations. He had entrusted to them the intimacies of His heart. And now His expectations were that He would be supported and stood by. He went through a great let-down.

Jesus gives us the key to dealing with the fickleness of friends and effectively handling the loneliness they cause. As the first reading says, we must turn to a Lord that is stable even when the whole world we live in seems to have fallen through. Jesus turns to His Father and, as Isaiah says, in the darkness of being alone, the Lord gives us a light. In the midst of enemies of all kinds, the Lord gives a sharp two-edged sword and a polished arrow.

Many of us look to other things than God's love for consolation in our loneliness. Some will drink, some will look to illicit, sexual love. Some will grovel in bitterness and some will give up entirely. Loneliness is a beautiful time to renew our faith in the personal love and concern that Jesus has for us right now. Jesus is God and is present to us from the moment of our conception. He's never left us. He's always there. We must reach out in faith and Christ will give us the victory over loneliness with a resurrection of love that has greater meaning and life, hope and sharing.

WEDNESDAY IN HOLY WEEK
Isaiah 50:4-9
Matthew 26:14-25

Jesus, Judas was a man that You had a special liking for. You chose him to be close to You. You could have picked others but You didn't because You really loved Judas. He let You down. Jesus, You love me. Like Judas, You've asked me to come and live with You, work with You and let You be the center of my life. Despite this overpowering love and special affection You've shown me, I know, deep down, that the plight of Judas can be mine. Help me to be careful with Your love for me. Don't let me cheat. Help me to run the race all the way to the end.

The Judas Possibility

From early childhood, I have seen Judas as the epitome of all that is bad and undesirable in a human being. When I first learned about Judas in school, he certainly wasn't the type of person you'd encourage your sister to go out with on a date. His life's end overshadowed any possibility of even his mother's loving him as a baby. Judas was the betrayer of Jesus and the greatest bad guy history has ever known.

The danger with finding Judas such a terrible person from his cradle to the hanging-tree is that he really doesn't have anything effective to say to me in my relationship with Jesus. We might have a problem with loving ourselves as we should but we would have to really be bottom man on the totem pole to find ourselves of the same caliber as Judas, thanks to his terrible press.

Unless we see good in Judas, he becomes unreal. He isn't a person who lived in the same world you and I live in. Unless we are honest in our understanding of Judas, the devil can make Judas into such a villain we can't believe his actions possible in our lives.

Judas was real. He was a great person too. Why? Because he was loved by Jesus in such a special way. Think of it!

Judas was one of the twelve Apostles. Now Jesus picked His Apostles for a very positive purpose. Jesus saw in each of them a potential for the spreading of His Kingdom. Judas was one of a very select few. Jesus had a special attraction for Judas. He wanted Judas to be close to Him for three whole years.

When we start to digest the fact that he was loved so much by Jesus, Judas starts to take on a new and vital life and possibility. He was a real person who felt and thought about the same things I do. He was a person of vision. He wanted things to change and he was willing to do something about it. He was willing to give three years of his life to living and working with Jesus.

The important thing to remember is that Judas has a strong similarity to you and me. Just as Judas was specially chosen by Jesus, so you and I, who have been baptized and have given our whole selves to Him, are chosen over many. We have been asked to live intimately with Him for more than the three years Judas was with Christ. Today we need to reflect on the possibility of turning away from Jesus. What can we do to ensure that what happened to Judas won't happen to us because, if we are honest, we know it can!

First, we must make sure that there is a continual communication going on between Jesus and us. That doesn't mean only coming to Him with adoration, contrition, thanksgiving and petitions. Along with that we must take the time to listen to His communication with us. We must be open to His direction. This means we must honestly face the evil that is moving in our lives and turn our backs on it. Now! This won't be easy to begin, but, through the power of Jesus, the completion will be a victory of joy.

Next we must read Scripture regularly. The power of God's word must permeate our lives. Jesus lives now through the Scriptures. Then, as a fruit of this deepening love-relationship, we must again and again step out in witnessing Jesus to the people who live in our world. I don't mean just pious platitudes about how to live a good life or how to be mentally healthy.

What I'm talking about is a courageous step out in faith to let the love we have for Jesus be the center of solutions to problems others come to us with.

Judas was not always the betrayer. He was a good man who was deeply loved by Jesus. But Judas gave up the struggle to make love grow. Ask any married couple about how love grows. There is a struggle to make relationships develop. As soon as we stop working and building, corruption sets in.

In a few days, during the Easter Vigil Service, we're going to be renewing our baptismal vows. Let's start the preparation for this today. Let's really make that dedication something special. Where we have slackened off in building our love for Jesus, let's resolve to take up the work and the fight anew, always aware that up to his betrayal, Judas was just as blessed as we are.

HOLY THURSDAY
Exodus 12:1-8, 11-14
1 *Corinthians* 11:23-26
John 13:1-15

Jesus, today You touch the heart of what love is all about. You give Yourself to us in the Eucharist. Help me to follow Your example and now give myself in service to those who need me. Give me the strength, through the Eucharist, to never grow tired of loving, especially those I don't like. May Your Heavenly Food help me to grow to an ever greater understanding of love.

The Eucharist, an on-Going Meal

Have you ever thought how central food is to the accounts of the Four Evangelists? Again and again we find Jesus concerned with feeding others or having a good meal Himself. Think about some of the times: when Mary washed His feet, He was eating; after He called Matthew, He was eating; His first miracle was at the wedding feast of Cana; when He cured Peter's mother-in-law, she got up and began serving Him food. Remember when His enemies were upset because His followers didn't fast like the followers of John? Jesus said they would fast after He was gone. With the Disciples at Emmaus, they knew Him in the breaking of bread. When He appeared to the Apostles on the shore after the Resurrection, He was cooking fish and then eating with them. He was very conscious of others getting enough to eat. He fed the 5,000. When He raised the little girl from the dead, one of His first instructions was to get her something to eat! The culmination of all this is seen in today's liturgy, when He gives us His very self in the Eucharist. Christ desires to be with us continually in the banquet of His love! What great importance meals have in Jesus' attempt to bring about His Kingdom.

What is it about meals that they play such a prominent place in the Christian message? Ideally, meals should be a time of union. One dish is shared by many people. Hopefully, there's a common table around which people are forced to stop and look at each other and get a chance to talk. A meal should be a slow-down time. A meal should make us relax and realize our bond of unity. I know this is speaking idealistically! In our hectic and rushing society, meals develop just the opposite of unity. In a big family, there are six different schedules, and eating together is next to impossible. Drive-in ordering snack-bars and quick service eat-as-you-run arrangements are great for fostering indigestion—the opposite of what Christ was aiming for when He stressed the importance of meals.

We have to do all in our power to make every meal that we eat something special. Every meal, whether it's donuts and coffee at work, a pizza and beer after a ball game, a family supper on a week night or a banquet on a big anniversary, has to be considered an integral part of our sharing of the Eucharist celebration.

All too often the Eucharist is seen as an oasis isolated from what we do all the rest of our time. Christ wants us to find Him again and again in all the things we do during our day to day, even menial, activities.

We must remind ourselves at every sharing of food that we are preparing for the Eucharist. The Eucharist is a celebration of reconciliation, sacrifice, communion, fellowship and love. This doesn't happen by magic. Our meals prior to the Eucharist must be a preparation for this.

One of the biggest difficulties with the Eucharist as celebrated in so many of our large parishes is that there are so many strangers sharing Communion. We must do everything we can to get to know as many people as we can in our parish. This is a big order, but it's a direction we must put great effort into. Fellowship meals should occur so that Communion at the Eucharist can take on the unity it is meant to.

I have heard several people say they don't come to the Eucharist anymore because they don't get anything out of it! The problem this betrays is one of a person expecting some kind of a performance that's aiming to entertain. The Eucharist is not a passive experience. The Eucharist demands preparation work on our part. We should have reflected on the readings before we came. We should do what we can to help with the singing preparation. But even more important than that, we should find the Eucharist as the culmination of a day or week of fostering unity, sacrifice, reconciliation and communion with members of our family and parish. The stress should not be what we get out of the Eucharist but rather what we contribute to this Meal of meals!

GOOD FRIDAY
Isaiah 52:13-53, 12
Hebrews 4:14-16; 5, 7-9
John 18:1-19, 42

Jesus, I've looked at You hanging on the cross so many times in my life that I take what happened that day, two centuries ago, a little for granted. At times, I can get so filled with the wonder of the Resurrection, that I fail to see today as a real possibility. Help me today to understand more the terrible reality of Your death. Deep in my heart, I know that since I've given my life to You, I must be willing to embrace Your death. Thank You for not holding back in Your desire to be totally human, to relate to me completely. I love You for this!

Jesus' Thoughts at His Death!

Good Friday is a difficult event to relate to with feelings akin to those of Jesus on that day 2,000 years ago, because we know what happened on the third day. Certainly Good Friday must have been a horrendous and emotion-packed day. But I know that Easter is coming and that although this day was bad, there forever is going to be the Easter sun peeping through the gloomiest day.

We must not so easily sweep Good Friday under the rug as a day of memorial before the inevitable victory. Good Friday is a reality today! We must try to touch in a new way what happened those many years ago and know that we're going to experience a similar suffering and death, since we have chosen to follow Christ. This is what the Body of Christ is all about. Jesus is alive today just as He was 2,000 years ago, and is living and dying and coming to life.

Let's think about what Jesus must have experienced as He hung dying on the cross on the hill outside the walls of Jerusalem.

Pain was very much on the mind of Jesus. There was the pulling pain of nails going through His hands and feet. The sore was opened and needing attention, but that wasn't possible

because there was the constant pressure the weight of His Body
was exerting, worsening the wounds. Then there was the pain
in His back. Externally there were the stripes from the whipping.
Added to this was the pain of the muscles that couldn't relax
because they were trying to relieve the pressure on the hands
and feet at the same time. Then there was a crown of thorns
which by now must have been throbbing with pain. He wanted
to lower His head and let it rest on His chest, but that was
impossible because when He did He found that He was con-
stricting His lungs and He couldn't breathe. Added to this was
a great dryness in His mouth due to the steady flow of blood
oozing from His body.

Next, Jesus felt heart-rending embarrassment. How sensitive we all are to having privacy. And here is Jesus, arms and
legs pinned, His body exposed to nakedness. He has nothing
He can call His own.

We think often of the anguish that Mary suffered at the
inhumanity inflicted upon her Son. This is so very true. As
we look at Mary's heartbreak and love we see such a beautiful
model of how we should grow in the love of Jesus. But let's
look at Mary's anguish from another viewpoint—Jesus'. Jesus
had a great love for Mary. We see this in His solicitude to
have John take care of her. What a terrible anguish Jesus must
have felt when He saw the helplessness and sorrow of His
Mother. How many times has a brave man, in our day, faltered
in risking his life, not because of cowardice but because of
the pain his death would cause to those he left behind? So
with Jesus, His heart was full of love for Mary. There's a
haunting Negro spiritual that touches this feeling. One verse
goes, "I think I heard him say, when he was given up the fight,
I think I heard him say, take my mother home!" When someone was as full of love as Jesus, the greatest torment could be
to hurt someone that He loved so very much. He was concerned that the Apostles wouldn't have to suffer with Him.
"If you are looking for Me, let these go their way." He loved
them too much to have them suffer too, as could have easily

been the case. But here was the most special woman of all His creations. Here was the vessel that bore God in her womb. Here was the Immaculate Spouse of the Holy Spirit. Here was the woman full of grace. And He knew that what was happening to Him was hurting her. He knew, as she had stroked His skin with the tenderness of every mother as she fondles her infant, her eyes now stroke every ugly gash on her Son's Body. Mary's sorrow was to Jesus a pain worse than the thorns or the nails or the slashes over His body.

In all of this the greatest suffering was that He had no recourse. "My God, My God, why have You forsaken Me?" Throughout the Gospels, Jesus is continually praying and relying on His Father. And now even this is gone. How can you say in words what the experience of being alone must have been like? Nothing! Nothing can be compared to this aloneness! We can only look on in wonder and reflect on such things as a woman losing a husband after thirty-five years of marriage, a prisoner unjustly condemned to life imprisonment and no courts of appeal—no escape from injustice!

Certainly Jesus has died once and for all and will never die again. But we, who are His Body today, know that just as His Resurrection must be made real in our lives, so also must His Death. This means we will be acquainted with pain, embarrassment, heartbreak and loneliness that are unbearable because God seems to have given up His support. Jesus' death should be cherished in all its aspects in our lives today.

EASTER

Jesus, Easter means life. You were dead, but now, You are alive again. You are the hope of my life! Death is a thing that I experience frequently in my life. I become dead to the person that I know I should be; I fall short of the dream that You have given me about myself. Then I become dead to other people. Somehow communication stops and antagonisms build until I'm dead in my relationship with You. I begin finding answers to life in things other than You. I let up on prayer; I rely on my own power to effect happiness, and soon I find that You have slipped out of my life. You are dead to me. Thank You for today Jesus. Today, I know that I have conquered any death to myself, others and You. Because You have come back from the dead, so have I. Thank you!

Easter Life Is Now

The resurrection of Jesus is a now experience. The resurrection's effectiveness is not found for us in fond recollections of what happened almost 2,000 years ago. The resurrection is a now experience in you and me! We are living three types of death from which the power of Jesus' resurrection can call us to life. The rays of the Easter Sun shoot their warmth and life into the dead relationships we experience with ourselves, others and God.

From Death to Self to Life

Deep, sometimes very deep, there is a dream of the great person that we can become. This dream we have of ourselves has dimmed. We know that if we can at least strive for our goal we will be happy, but death is a force that stops our striving and we allow ourselves to be satisfied with second best. We allow ourselves to just be content with getting along. We are separated from the dream of our lives.

And then the resurrection happens. Suddenly in the depth of our estrangement, we come to the awareness that God loves us in a personal and real and strong way. And we reach out and start to make the dream we have been entrusted with by God something tangible. We start to cultivate the talents we have and develop an art we knew we had if we just took the time to practice. We start in school again to get the education that will be the key to effectively helping others. We start to pray and thus come closer to the ground of our being. We start to reach beyond what we are confident that we can do and begin to touch extreme possibilities. We start liking ourselves!

This is what the resurrection means. This is the new life that we take on when we start to live the life of Christ. We pass over from death to life when we start to grow into the persons that we know we can be.

From Death to Others to Life

Many times we are dead to other people. Relationships have been cut off. Perhaps we ignore another or we treat him with extreme tolerance or we are vehemently against him and might even move to the extent of violence. The relationship with another person is dead. There might even be this relationship of separations from a person that we have committed ourselves to. Perhaps a husband is dead to his wife. Divorce is being contemplated as the best thing for the children. The angry silence is becoming detrimental to everyone.

And then the resurrection happens. For some unexplainable reason, life comes to the relationship. There is communication. There is hope. There are real concrete actions being taken to bring about something new and alive. This is what the power of Jesus in His resurrection is all about. Marriages that are dead are brought to life. Employees who have no respect for their employers suddenly are aware of goodness in their bosses. Prejudice is honestly examined and barriers begin to fall. Friendships are fostered where they had never seemed possible. Resurrection means new life with those who were dead to us.

From Death to God to Life

Finally we can be dead to God. Perhaps the fervor that had been ours when we were children has slowly died through the concerns we have that take up all our time: relationships, money, esteem, money, relaxation, money, vocation and money. And in the process God is someone that doesn't really have a place in our lives except for occasional church functions. And then something happens. The grace of God moves in a mysterious way in our lives and suddenly we are alive to God. He is real. He is someone we can love with all our hearts, and we are willing to give Him everything we have. Jesus is no longer a person we look upon as an historical character similar to Socrates. Jesus is alive right now moving with a driving force in the midst of everything we do or are concerned with. Jesus lives and is my hope and my joy. I share with Him a life that will never end. And a life that will never end is what being a follower of Jesus is all about!

Have a happy new life in Jesus!

An Interesting Thought

The publication you have just finished reading is part of the apostolic efforts of the Society of St. Paul of the American Province. A small, unique group of priests and brothers, the members of the Society of St. Paul propose to bring the message of Christ to men through the communications media while living the religious life.

If you know of a young man who might be interested in learning more about our life and mission, ask him to contact the Vocation Office in care of ALBA HOUSE, at 2187 Victory Blvd., Staten Island, New York 10314. Full information will be sent without cost or obligation. You may be instrumental in helping a young man to find his vocation in life. *An interesting thought.*